A KID'S GUIDE TO FOOTBALL LEGENDS

HAIL MARYS, HISTORY AND INSPIRING STORIES FROM THE GRIDIRON

KENT JAMESON

Published by:
Kent Jameson Publishing
kentjamesonpublishing@gmail.com
Printed in the United States of America.
First Printing, 2024
Library of Congress Cataloging-in-Publication Data:
Kent Jameson
A Kid's Guide To Football Legends: Hail Marys, History and Inspiring Stories from the Gridiron

TABLE OF CONTENTS

INTRODUCTION

Did you know that the longest recorded field goal in NFL history is 66 yards? Justin Tucker of the Baltimore Ravens set this record in 2021. He kicked the ball with precision and power, sending it soaring through the air and right between the uprights. The crowd roared. The players celebrated. Moments like this are what make football so exciting and unforgettable.

Welcome to a world where every game is a new adventure. This book is designed for you—kids aged 7 to 17—who want to learn more about football. Whether you're new to the game or already a big fan, you'll find stories here that are both inspiring and fun. You'll learn about the birth of this incredible sport and its evolution over the years. We'll cover thrilling moments and the legends who have left their mark on the field.

Football is more than just a game. It's a part of American culture. It brings people together. Families gather to watch their favorite teams. Friends cheer and celebrate together. Football has a rich history, filled with great players and unforgettable moments. It's a sport that teaches teamwork, perseverance, and passion.

In this book, you'll find a variety of chapters that will guide you through different aspects of the game. We'll start with the birth of football and how it has changed over time. You'll learn the basics of the game, from the terminology to the uniforms. We'll introduce you to some of the greatest players ever, like Tom Brady, and those who are considered modern-day icons. We'll also talk about the giants of the game, known for their impressive size and strength, and the defensive dynamos who have stopped even the best offenses.

We'll honor the pioneers who helped shape the game. We'll spotlight rising stars who are making their mark today. You'll read about famous matchups and rivalries that keep fans on the edge of their seats. We'll relive some of the greatest moments in football history, like The Immaculate Reception and The Catch. Finally, we'll share inspirational tales from the gridiron that show the heart and soul of the game.

This book caters to young readers with a passion for football. It's for those who are just getting to know the sport and for those who have loved it for years. We've included interactive elements to make learning fun. You'll see a blend of fiction with reality, bringing stories to life in a way that no other book does.

I'm thrilled to share my passion for football with you. I've spent years watching games, studying players, and learning the history of football. I want to make the sport accessible and enjoyable for you. My goal is to help you understand and appreciate the game just as much as I do.

So, are you ready to dive into the thrilling world of football? Join me on this exciting journey. You'll discover the stories behind the legends and learn what makes this sport so special. By the end, you'll not only gain knowledge but also find inspiration in the tales of courage and determination on the field. Let's get started!

CHAPTER 1
THE BIRTH OF FOOTBALL

Have you ever wondered how football, that thrilling game played in packed stadiums, first began? It didn't start with roaring crowds or Super Bowls. Long before quarterbacks threw perfect spirals or receivers made jaw-dropping catches, the seeds of football were planted in ancient times. The game we love has roots that stretch back thousands of years, across many countries and cultures. This chapter will uncover the journey from ancient ball games to the creation of football. It's a story full of surprising twists, smart innovations, and a few quirky characters.

1.1 THE HUMBLE BEGINNINGS: FOOTBALL'S ANCESTRY

Long before modern football, people played a game called "Episkyros" in ancient Greece. This game involved two teams trying to throw a ball over the other team's line. It was fast-paced and fun, much like the football we know today. Players would gather in open fields, and their goal was simple: get the ball to the other side. The rules were not as strict, and the play was often rough. But it set the stage for what would eventually become the sport we now cheer for every Sunday.

As centuries passed, people in medieval Europe developed their own version of football. Villages would compete in a rough and tumble game that often took over entire towns. The game had few rules. Players would kick, throw, and run with the ball, trying to reach a goal. These games were chaotic. Yet, they were filled with energy and excitement. They were a social event, bringing communities together. These early games laid the groundwork for the more organized versions that followed.

Fast forward to the 19th century in America. College students began playing their own style of football. One of the earliest recorded matches was between Rutgers and Princeton in 1869. This game borrowed elements from both rugby and soccer. It marked a turning point, as it was the first step toward the football we recognize today. The rules were a mix of different sports, and players mostly kicked the ball. But it was a start. It captured the attention of many, and soon more schools began to form their own teams.

Walter Camp, often called the "Father of American Football," played a crucial role in shaping the game. He introduced important changes that made the sport unique. He created the line of scrimmage, where each play begins, and the system of downs, which gives teams four chances to move the ball ten yards. These innovations transformed the game from a chaotic scramble into a strategic battle. Camp's ideas helped football grow into a popular college sport. His influence is still felt today, as his rules form the backbone of modern football.

Rugby and soccer also played a part in the evolution of football. Rugby contributed the idea of tackling and the physical side of the game. Soccer influenced the use of kicking and the concept of moving the ball downfield. These sports helped shape early football rules. They introduced the idea of teams working together to score points. Over time, American football developed its own identity. It blended these influences into something new and exciting.

As college football grew in popularity, the idea of playing football professionally began to take shape. College games drew large crowds, and the excitement was contagious. People started to see the potential for a professional league. This shift marked the beginning of football as a national pastime. Players were eager to showcase their skills, and fans loved the thrill of the game. The foundation was laid for football to grow into the beloved sport it is today.

1.2 THE FIRST KICKOFF: BIRTH OF THE NFL

In the fall of 1920, a group of men met in a small, cozy room in Canton, Ohio. The room belonged to Ralph Hay, who owned a local football team called the Canton Bulldogs. They gathered in an auto showroom surrounded by shiny cars, but their minds were on something far bigger. They wanted to create a league that would bring together the best football teams in the country. This bold idea led to the birth of what we now know as the National Football League, or NFL. At first, they called it the American Professional Football Association. Eleven teams joined this new league, including the Akron Pros, Dayton Triangles, and Decatur Staleys. These teams were the first to step into this new world of professional football, hoping to build something lasting and exciting.

However, the road ahead was not easy. The early NFL faced many challenges. Money was tight, and teams struggled to stay afloat. Back then, college football was king. It had big crowds and lots of fans, while the NFL was just getting started. Many people thought professional football would never catch on. It was hard for the league to compete with the popularity of college teams. Teams also had trouble finding good players and keeping them. Some players would switch teams for a better offer, and there were no strict rules to stop them. Despite these obstacles, the league pressed forward, driven by a dream of making football a beloved sport across the nation.

Key figures played important roles in the growth and stability of the NFL during these early years. Among them was George Halas, who was not only a player and coach but also a team owner. He was deeply committed to the league's success. Halas helped to shape the rules and promote the game to fans everywhere. His team, the Decatur Staleys, later became the Chicago Bears, one of the NFL's most storied franchises. Another important figure was Jim Thorpe, an incredible athlete who became the league's first president. Thorpe was already famous for his achievements in track and field, and his involvement brought credibility and attention to the fledgling league. His leadership helped set the foundation for the league's future.

As the NFL continued to grow, more teams joined the ranks, and the league began to organize its structure. The league introduced rules to ensure fair play and competition. Over time, they standardized the playing field and equipment, which helped make games safer and more exciting. Teams from different regions of the country joined, bringing more diversity and talent to the league. The NFL started to gain a following as fans began to take notice of this exciting new brand of football. The league's expansion helped it gain credibility and a larger audience.

The NFL's growth was not just about adding more teams. It was also about creating a sense of community and tradition. Teams developed fierce rivalries and loyal fan bases. Games were more than just matches; they were events that brought people together. Fans cheered for their teams with passion and pride. The league's popularity soared as more people discovered the thrill of NFL football. The NFL began to capture the imagination of the public, offering something unique and thrilling. As it grew, the league set the stage for what would become one of the most beloved sports in America.

1.3 EVOLUTION OF THE GAME: FROM LEATHER HELMETS TO HIGH TECH

Imagine stepping onto the field with nothing but a leather cap on your head. That's how the earliest football players protected themselves. In those days, helmets were made of soft leather. They offered little protection against the rough tackles and hard knocks of the game. Players often left the field with bruises and cuts. As the sport grew, so did the need for better safety gear. This led to the development of plastic helmets in the mid-20th century. These helmets were stronger and could better absorb impact, which helped protect players from serious injuries. Today, helmets are marvels of technology. They include advanced padding, face masks, and even sensors to measure hits. Engineers and scientists work tirelessly to improve safety features, ensuring that players are well-protected while playing the game they love.

Protective padding has also come a long way. Early football players had little more than heavy woolen shirts to cushion them. It was not until the 1950s that shoulder pads made of foam and plastic became standard. These pads offered significant protection, allowing players to tackle and block more aggressively without fear of injury. Over time, additional padding for thighs, knees, and elbows was introduced. Today's equipment is lightweight yet incredibly strong. It is designed to absorb the force of a hit and distribute it evenly across the body. This means players can focus on their game without worrying about getting hurt. The evolution of protective gear has made football safer and more enjoyable for players at all levels.

Technology has changed football in other ways, too. Instant replay and video technology have transformed officiating. In the past, referees had to make split-second decisions with no second chances. Mistakes were hard to correct, and controversial calls could change the outcome of a game. Now, with high-definition cameras capturing every angle, officials can review plays and make more accurate calls. This ensures fair play and helps maintain the integrity of the game. The development of synthetic turf has also revolutionized football fields. Unlike natural grass, synthetic turf is durable and can withstand heavy use without becoming damaged. It provides a consistent playing surface, reducing the risk of slips and falls. Players can perform at their best, knowing the field is safe and reliable.

Training and fitness have become key parts of a football player's life. In the early days, players kept in shape through basic exercises and drills. Today, they follow detailed training plans that include strength, speed, and agility workouts. Nutrition plays a big role, too. Players eat balanced diets to fuel their bodies and recover quickly from games. Sports science has introduced new methods for conditioning, like using data to track performance and tailor workouts to individual needs. This scientific approach ensures that players are in peak condition. It helps them stay healthy throughout the long and demanding football season.

These changes have had a profound impact on the way football is played. The game is faster and more dynamic than ever before. Players are stronger and more agile, able to execute complex plays with precision. Coaches can develop intricate strategies that take advantage of their players' skills. This has led to thrilling games full of excitement and surprises. Fans watch in awe as players make incredible catches, break through defenses, and score impossible touchdowns. The evolution of equipment, technology, and training has elevated football to new heights, making it a spectacular sport that continues to capture the hearts of millions around the world.

Quick Quiz: Evolution of Football

Think about how much football has changed over the years. Test your knowledge with this quick quiz! What were the earliest football helmets made from? How have instant replays improved officiating? What is one key difference between natural grass and synthetic turf? How has nutrition become important for modern players? Take a moment to jot down your answers and see how much you've learned about the evolution of this amazing sport.

1.4 ICONIC CHANGES: HOW THE RULES SHAPED THE GAME

In the early days of football, the game was quite different. One of the most important changes came with the introduction of the forward pass. Before this, players mostly ran with the ball or kicked it to move it downfield. The forward pass allowed quarterbacks to throw the ball to receivers farther away, opening up new strategies and making the game more dynamic. This change added excitement and unpredictability to football. Teams could score more easily and quickly, which thrilled fans. Coaches began to build their teams around skilled passers and fast receivers, creating the high-scoring games we love today.

Another major rule change was the introduction of the modern scoring system. In the early years, scoring was inconsistent. Points were awarded differently, and it was hard to keep track of who was winning. The new system standardized scoring, making it easier for fans to follow games. Touchdowns became worth six points, with extra points and field goals adding to the score. This change made games more thrilling, as teams could come from behind with a single big play. It also encouraged teams to develop diverse offensive strategies, balancing running and passing to outscore their opponents.

As the rules evolved, so did the strategies. Coaches began to use the spread offense, which spread players across the field to create space and confuse defenses. This strategy relies on quick passes and agile receivers to move the ball quickly. It forces defenses to cover more ground, creating opportunities for big plays. Another strategic change was the no-huddle offense. Teams used this to keep defenses on their toes, preventing them from substituting players or catching their breath. By keeping up the pace, offenses could control the tempo of the game and wear down their opponents. These strategies have become key in modern football, making games faster and more exciting.

Player safety has always been a concern, leading to important rule changes. One significant rule is the helmet-to-helmet contact regulation. This rule prevents players from making dangerous tackles that could cause head injuries. It aims to protect players and reduce the risk of concussions. The NFL has also introduced other safety rules, like those protecting quarterbacks from late hits. These changes ensure that while the game remains tough and competitive, it does not put players in unnecessary danger. By focusing on safety, the NFL shows its commitment to player health, making the game safer for everyone involved.

The NFL Competition Committee plays a vital role in these rule changes. This group of experts reviews the game and suggests improvements. They analyze how rules affect gameplay and make recommendations to enhance safety and fairness. The committee includes coaches, team owners, and other football experts. They meet annually to discuss potential changes and consider feedback from players and fans. Their work helps the NFL evolve, keeping the game fresh and exciting while maintaining its core values. The committee's efforts ensure that rules are fair and reflect the current state of the game.

As we look back at these iconic changes, it's clear that rules have shaped football into the thrilling sport it is today. The introduction of the forward pass and modern scoring system transformed how teams play. New strategies like the spread and no-huddle offenses keep fans on the edge of their seats. Safety rules protect players, allowing them to compete at their best without fear of injury. The

NFL Competition Committee ensures that the game continues to grow and improve. These changes have not only made the game more exciting but also more inclusive and safe. Football remains a sport that captures the imagination of fans young and old. As the game continues to evolve, its rich history and dynamic nature promise a future filled with even more iconic moments.

CHAPTER 2
UNDERSTANDING THE GAME

2.1 LINGO ON THE FIELD: TEAMS TERMS MADE EASY

In football, every play is a puzzle, and language is the key to solving it. The sport has its own set of words and phrases that might seem confusing at first. But once you learn them, you'll see the game in a whole new way. These terms help players communicate quickly and clearly, making it easier to work together and execute their strategies.

Let's start with one of the most exciting words in football: "Touchdown." When a player carries, catches, or recovers the ball in the opposing team's end zone, this is called a touchdown. It earns the team six points. A touchdown is always a thrilling moment. Fans jump to their feet, and teammates celebrate. It's the ultimate goal for the offense. You'll hear the word a lot during games, as scoring is the main aim. Another key term is "Interception." It happens when a defensive player catches a pass meant for an offensive player. Imagine a quarterback throwing the ball to a receiver, but a defender leaps in, snatching it away. This can change the flow of the game, giving the defensive team a chance to go on the attack.

Football has its own jargon, and understanding it helps you follow the game better. Take "Blitz," for example, which is a defensive tactic. When the defense wants to put extra pressure on the quarterback, they send more players to rush him. This is called a blitz. It's a risky move because it leaves fewer players to cover the receivers. But if timed well, it can disrupt the offense and lead to a sack or interception. "Hail Mary" is another term you might hear. It describes a long, desperate pass thrown by the quarterback, usually at the end of a game when a team needs a miracle to win. It's named after the prayer, as it often relies on hope and luck.

Scoring in football involves more than just touchdowns. You might hear about a "Field Goal." This is when the team kicks the ball through the goalposts, earning three points. It's a valuable way to score, especially when a touchdown seems out of reach. After a touchdown, teams can also try for an "Extra Point" by kicking the ball through the posts for one point. Alternatively, they might attempt a two-point conversion by running or passing the ball into the end zone again. These options add strategy to the game and can be crucial in close matches.

Let's talk about the "Pocket." It's not an actual pocket but a safe area where the quarterback stands while looking to pass the ball. The offensive line creates this protective space, shielding the quarterback from defenders. Picture a bubble around him, with linemen forming a wall to keep the defense at bay. If the pocket collapses, the quarterback must react quickly, either by throwing the ball or running to escape pressure. This term helps you visualize the action and understand the quarterback's role.

Quick Quiz: Know Your Football Terms

Think you've got the hang of football lingo? Test your knowledge with this quick quiz! What happens during a blitz? How many points is a field goal worth? What's the pocket in football? Take a moment to write down your answers. See how well you understand these key terms that make the game so exciting.

2.2 GAMEDAY GEAR: UNIFORMS AND EQUIPMENT EXPLAINED

When players step onto the field, they wear special gear that keeps them safe and helps them perform their best. The uniform is more than just a team jersey and pants. It's designed to protect players from the intense physical contact that happens in every game. At the top of this list is the helmet. Made from hard plastic, the helmet shields the head from impacts. Inside, padding cushions the skull, reducing the risk of injury. Helmets also have face masks made of metal bars. They protect the face while allowing the player to see clearly. Visors can be added to shield the eyes from sunlight and glare. These features combined make the helmet a crucial piece of safety equipment.

Shoulder pads are another important part of the uniform. They sit on top of a player's shoulders and chest, made from foam and plastic. These pads absorb the shocks and hits players take during the game. They spread the force over a larger area, which helps prevent injuries. Shoulder pads allow players to tackle and block with less risk. Despite their size, they are lightweight, letting players move freely. The design of shoulder pads has improved over the years. They are now more comfortable and better at protecting players, allowing them to focus on the game.

Cleats are the shoes that players wear. They have special spikes on the bottom. These spikes dig into the grass or turf, giving players better traction. This grip helps players run faster and turn quickly without slipping. Cleats come in different styles, depending on the playing surface. For example, some are made for natural grass, while others are for artificial turf. The right pair of cleats can make a big difference in a player's performance. They provide stability, helping players stay balanced during fast-paced action.

Some players use specialized gear to help them with their roles on the team. Quarterbacks often wear wristbands with play calls printed on them. This handy tool helps them remember the plays during the game. They can quickly check their wristband to see the next move. This way, they don't have to memorize everything or worry about forgetting key plays. Wristbands are a simple yet effective way to keep the game plan on track. They help quarterbacks stay focused and lead their team with confidence.

Football equipment has seen many innovations over the years. One of the latest advancements is the use of GPS trackers. These small devices are worn by players during practice and games. They help coaches track the movements and speed of each player. By analyzing this data, coaches can tailor training programs to improve performance. GPS trackers also monitor player fatigue, helping teams prevent injuries. This technology is changing how teams prepare for games. It gives coaches and players valuable insights to stay competitive.

The gear players wear is more than just protection. It enhances their ability to play at high levels. Every piece of equipment has a purpose, from the helmet down to the cleats. The advancements in technology make these tools better every year. Players can rely on their gear to keep them safe and give them an edge on the field.

2.3 POSITIONS AND ROLES: WHO DOES WHAT ON THE FIELD?

In football, each player has a specific job that helps the team. The offense is the side responsible for moving the ball forward and trying to score points. At the heart of this effort is the quarterback. The quarterback is like the team leader. They receive the snap from the center and decide whether to pass the ball to a receiver, hand it off to a running back, or keep it and run themselves. This role requires quick thinking and precise throws. The quarterback must read the defense and make smart choices under pressure. Their decisions can change the outcome of a game in an instant.

Behind the quarterback stands the running back. This player is key in advancing the ball on the ground. Running backs are known for their speed and agility. They take handoffs from the quarterback and try to gain as many yards as possible. They must dodge defenders, find open lanes, and sometimes catch passes. Running backs need to be tough and resilient, as they take hits from the defense. Their ability to break tackles and outrun opponents can turn a simple play into a spectacular touchdown.

Defense is all about stopping the offense from scoring. It requires a different set of skills and strategies. Linebackers are the versatile defenders who play a crucial role here. They line up behind the defensive line and are involved in many aspects of the game. They tackle running backs, rush the quarterback, and cover receivers. Linebackers need to be strong and fast to handle these varied tasks. They often serve as the defense's leaders, calling plays and adjusting positions based on what they see from the offense. Their ability to read the game and react quickly is vital.

Cornerbacks are another important part of the defense. Their main job is to cover wide receivers and stop them from catching passes. They need to be quick and agile to keep up with fast receivers. Cornerbacks must anticipate the quarterback's throws and have good timing to intercept or knock down passes. They are often the last line of defense, making crucial tackles to prevent big plays. Their ability to stick closely to receivers can make the difference between a completed pass and a turnover.

Special teams come into play during kicking situations. These players might not be on the field as often, but their roles are just as important. Kickers are responsible for field goals and extra points. Their accuracy can win games, especially when the score is close. Punters, on the other hand, kick the ball away on fourth down to give the opposing team the ball as far back as possible. Their ability to control the distance and placement of the ball affects field position, which is a strategic part of the game. Special teams players must stay focused and ready, as they often have just one chance to make a big impact.

All these positions work together like pieces of a puzzle. The offensive line is crucial in protecting the quarterback. These players form a barrier to stop defenders from reaching the quarterback. They open up paths for running backs and give the quarterback time to throw. Without a strong offensive line, the offense would struggle to gain yards. The teamwork between the line, quarterback, and running backs is essential for a successful offense. On defense, players communicate and adjust based on the offense's actions. They must trust each other to cover their assignments and react quickly to changes. This teamwork creates a cohesive unit that can thwart even the most skilled offenses. Each player's role is vital. Their combined efforts create the exciting and dynamic game of football that fans love.

2.4 STRATEGY BASICS: PLAYS AND FORMATIONS DEMYSTIFIED

Football is a game of strategy. Teams use different plays and formations to outsmart their opponents. These strategies help them move the ball down the field and score points. On offense, two fundamental plays are the "Run" and the "Pass." Each has its own strengths and purposes. A "Run" play involves handing the ball to a running back, who then charges forward, trying to gain as many yards as possible. These plays are powerful and help control the clock. They are also safer because there is less chance of losing the ball. On the other hand, "Pass" plays involve the quarterback throwing the ball to a receiver. These plays can cover more ground quickly and are great for surprising the defense. But they also carry a risk of interception if the defense catches the ball instead. Teams choose between these plays based on their goals and the defense's weaknesses.

One special type of pass play is the "Screen Pass." This play involves the quarterback quickly throwing the ball to a receiver or running back behind the line of scrimmage. The offensive line then moves forward to block defenders. This creates a protective wall for the player with the ball. The screen pass can catch the defense off guard, especially when they expect a deep pass. It's a clever tactic that can lead to big gains if executed well. Teams use it to slow down aggressive defenses and gain valuable yards.

Defensive formations are all about stopping the offense. Two common formations are the "4-3 defense" and the "3-4 defense." The "4-3 defense" uses four defensive linemen and three linebackers. This formation is strong against the run. The linemen tackle the running back, while the linebackers cover the rest of the field. It's a balanced setup, good for both stopping runs and pressuring the quarterback. The "3-4 defense" has three linemen and four linebackers. It offers more flexibility, allowing for creative blitzes. The extra linebacker can either rush the quarterback or drop back to cover a receiver. This unpredictability makes it harder for the offense to plan their moves.

Special teams have their own strategies, especially during kicking plays. One exciting tactic is the "Onside Kick." This is used when a team kicks the ball short intentionally, hoping to recover it themselves. It's a risky play, often used when a team is behind and needs to score quickly. The kicker tries to make the ball bounce unpredictably, giving their teammates a chance to grab it before the opposing team does. It can turn the tide of a game, but if it fails, it gives the other team good field position.

Visualizing plays can help you understand them better. Picture a "Shotgun formation," where the quarterback stands several yards behind the center, ready to receive the snap. This position allows them more time to spot open receivers or hand off the ball to a running back. It's often used in passing situations to give the quarterback a clear view of the field. Now consider a "Zone defense." In this setup, defensive players cover specific areas of the field rather than sticking to one opponent. They watch the quarterback's eyes and react to the ball. This strategy can confuse quarterbacks and lead to interceptions.

Understanding these strategies and formations is key to appreciating football. They show how teams think and adapt to different situations. Every play is a chance to gain an advantage and push toward victory. As you watch games, look for these elements in action. Notice how teams use them to create opportunities and stop their opponents. These tactics make football an exciting chess match on the field, where every move counts. With these strategies in mind, you are ready to explore even more about the amazing world of NFL football.

CHAPTER 3
THE LEGENDS OF
THE GAME

You've stepped onto a football field and hear the roar of thousands of fans. The pressure is intense, but you're ready. You're prepared to lead your team to victory. This is the world Tom Brady knows well. He is one of the greatest quarterbacks to ever play the game. Many call him the GOAT, which stands for "Greatest of All Time." But Brady's journey to this title wasn't easy. It's a story of hard work, determination, and overcoming the odds.

3.1 TOM BRADY: THE JOURNEY TO BECOMING GOAT

Tom Brady's path to NFL stardom began with challenges. In 2000, the New England Patriots drafted him as the 199th pick in the sixth round. This means many teams overlooked him. Scouts doubted his athletic ability. They questioned if he had the skills to succeed in the NFL. Brady had to prove them wrong. At the University of Michigan, he faced similar doubts. He shared playing time with another quarterback, Drew Henson. Brady learned patience and resilience. He worked tirelessly to improve his game.

Brady's career is full of impressive achievements. He has won seven Super Bowl titles, more than any other player in NFL history. He led the Patriots to six championships and the Tampa Bay Buccaneers to one. His Super Bowl wins include many unforgettable moments. Brady has also earned multiple NFL MVP awards. These honors recognize him as one of the league's best players. Through each season, he showed unmatched skill and leadership. His performances under pressure, like in Super Bowl comebacks, are legendary.

Brady's work ethic sets him apart. He follows a strict training routine, focusing on physical fitness and mental sharpness. He studies his opponents carefully. Brady also works on his throws, footwork, and decision-making. He constantly seeks ways to improve. His dedication inspires teammates and young athletes. He leads by example, showing that hard work pays off. In high-pressure situations, Brady remains calm and focused. This quality helps him make smart decisions when the game is on the line.

Tom Brady has changed how people see the quarterback position. He uses quick reads and precise throws to outsmart defenses. His ability to adapt to different styles of play has influenced coaches and players. Young quarterbacks look up to him. They try to learn from his techniques and strategies. Brady also shares his knowledge with others. He mentors younger players, helping them develop their skills. His leadership has set a high standard for what it means to be a quarterback.

Tom Brady's influence extends beyond his performance on the field. He has shown that perseverance and dedication can lead to greatness. His story is one of believing in oneself and never giving up. Despite early doubts and challenges, Brady rose to the top. He is a role model for anyone facing obstacles. His journey reminds us that success comes from hard work and determination. As you learn about his career, think about how you can apply these lessons to your own life.

Interactive Activity: Brady's Playbook

Imagine you're a quarterback like Tom Brady. Create your own playbook by drawing a play on a piece of paper. Think about the positions of your teammates. Decide if you want to run or pass the ball. Use arrows to show movement. Afterward, explain your strategy to a friend or family member. Discuss how your play might work against a defense. This activity helps you understand the planning and teamwork involved in football. It encourages you to think like a pro.

3.2 JERRY RICE: HANDS OF FAME

Jerry Rice stands out as one of the most exceptional wide receivers in NFL history. His ability to catch the football was nothing short of amazing. Imagine a football soaring through the air, and Rice snatching it with ease, no matter how difficult the pass. His hands seemed almost magnetic, drawing the ball in securely every time. This catching ability paired with his precise route running made him nearly unstoppable. Rice moved with grace and purpose, always finding the right path to evade defenders. He ran routes with the accuracy of a skilled artist drawing lines on a canvas. Defenders struggled to keep up with his sharp cuts and sudden bursts of speed. His work on the field was a testament to years of dedication and practice.

Jerry Rice's career is a tale of records and achievements. He holds the record for the most career receptions, yards, and touchdowns by a wide receiver. These records aren't just numbers; they represent years of consistent excellence. Rice played in the NFL for over two decades, maintaining top performance year after year. This consistency is rare and speaks to his unmatched work ethic. Rice practiced tirelessly, often arriving at the field before anyone else and leaving last. He believed that hard work would always beat talent when talent didn't work hard. His career serves as proof that dedication and effort can lead to extraordinary success.

Life wasn't always easy for Jerry. He faced challenges on his way to NFL stardom. Rice came from a small college, Mississippi Valley State University, which wasn't known for producing NFL stars. Many doubted if he could succeed in the professional league. But Rice never let those doubts stop him. He worked even harder to prove himself. His transition from a small college to the NFL was not just a leap in terms of skill level but also in the level of competition. He faced bigger, faster, and more experienced players. Yet, Rice rose to the challenge. His perseverance earned him a spot with the San Francisco 49ers, where he began to shine. Every setback became a stepping stone for greater achievements.

Jerry Rice's legacy goes beyond his records and awards. He has inspired countless young athletes to dream big and work hard. Aspiring wide receivers look up to him, hoping to emulate his success. Coaches use his techniques and strategies as teaching tools. Rice has contributed to the evolution of passing strategies in the game. His ability to create separation from defenders redefined how wide receivers are expected to play. The NFL today owes much of its passing success to players like Rice. They have shown that with the right skills and determination, anything is possible on the field.

Reflection: What Makes a Legend?

Think about Jerry Rice's story. What qualities helped him succeed? Was it his skill, hard work, or ability to overcome challenges? Take a moment to reflect on what makes someone a legend. Write down a few thoughts or discuss them with a friend. Consider how you can apply these qualities in your own life, whether in sports, school, or any other passion you pursue.

3.3 WALTER PAYTON: SWEETNESS AND STRENGTH

Walter Payton was a force of nature on the football field. His nickname, "Sweetness," seemed to capture both his playing style and his personality. Payton had an incredible ability to do it all. He wasn't just a great runner. He could also catch passes and block like a pro. This versatility made him a valuable player for the Chicago Bears. Payton could break through defenses with sheer power, but he was also nimble. He could dodge and weave like few others. His stamina was legendary. He played 13 seasons, rarely missing a game. Payton's endurance and skill set him apart from many other running backs of his time.

What made Payton truly special was his approach to life and football. He lived by the motto "Never Die Easy." This meant he always gave his best effort, no matter the situation. On the field, Payton would fight for every yard, refusing to go down without a challenge. Off the field, he carried this same determination into everything he did. Payton believed in striving for excellence and working as part of a team. He knew that success wasn't just about individual talent. It was about how well you could work with others. His commitment to these principles made him a respected leader both on and off the field.

Payton's career was filled with remarkable achievements. He won the NFL Most Valuable Player award, a testament to his skill and impact on the game. One of his most memorable contributions was leading the Chicago Bears to victory in Super Bowl XX. The Bears dominated the game, thanks in large part to Payton's efforts. Though he didn't score a touchdown in that game, his presence and skill helped the team secure the championship. Payton's career totals were astounding. He held the record for the most rushing yards at the time of his retirement. His talent and dedication left a lasting mark on the NFL.

Beyond his football achievements, Payton was known for his generosity and kindness. He dedicated much of his life to helping others. Payton established the Walter Payton Foundation, which focused on supporting underprivileged children and families. His work in the community was as impressive as his work on the field. The NFL honors his legacy with the Walter Payton Man of the Year Award. This award recognizes players who excel on the field and make significant contributions to their communities. Payton's commitment to giving back inspired many others to do the same.

Payton's influence extended far beyond the football field. He showed that greatness comes not just from talent but from heart

and determination. His story continues to inspire future generations of athletes and fans. Young players look up to his example,
striving to achieve both personal and team success. His legacy
reminds everyone that true strength comes from a blend of skill,
perseverance, and compassion. Walter Payton's life and career
demonstrate the powerful impact one person can have, both in
sports and in the broader world. His lessons of teamwork,
resilience, and charity remain relevant and inspiring to this day.

3.4 BEYOND THE FIELD: LIFE LESSONS FROM LEGENDS

In the world of football, the field is where players show their skills.
But the true legends are defined by more than their athletic abilities. They share common themes that inspire us all. Resilience and
dedication stand out among these traits. These athletes faced
tough times and challenges. Instead of giving up, they pushed
through to become the best. They never stopped growing. They
always looked for ways to improve, both on and off the field. This
dedication teaches us that success requires constant effort and a
willingness to learn. It's not about where you start. It's about
where you choose to go.

Sportsmanship is another key ingredient in the mix. These players
showed respect for their opponents, treating every game with
integrity. They understood that true competition isn't just about
winning. It's about playing fair and respecting everyone involved.
Even in the heat of the moment, they kept their cool. They didn't
let emotions take over. They played with honor and dignity. This
attitude set an example for teammates and fans alike. It showed
that being a good sport can make a big difference. It can turn a
regular game into an unforgettable experience for everyone
watching.

Off the field, these legends had a broader impact. They became role models for aspiring athletes and young fans. Kids looked up to them, not just for their skills but for their character. They inspired young people to dream big and work hard. This influence extended beyond sports. It touched every part of life. They showed that you can be successful and still be kind and humble. Their actions proved that greatness isn't just about what you achieve. It's about how you achieve it and the positive mark you leave on others.

Take, for instance, the stories of personal challenges they over-came. One player battled an injury that could have ended his career. Instead of giving up, he worked tirelessly to recover. His determination paid off. He returned to the field stronger than ever. Another legend faced criticism early in his career. People doubted his abilities. They said he wouldn't make it. But he used that doubt as fuel. He trained harder and proved everyone wrong. These stories remind us that setbacks are part of life. They show that what matters most is how you respond to them.

These players also showed leadership in their communities. They didn't just focus on football. They cared about making a difference. One player started a program to help kids stay active and healthy. Another dedicated time to visiting schools, encouraging students to pursue their dreams. They understood the power of giving back. They used their fame to support causes they believed in. Their efforts helped build stronger, healthier communities. They proved that leadership isn't just about being the best on the field. It's about using your influence for good.

As we look at these legends, we see a bigger picture. Their stories are about more than just football. They're about resilience, sports-manship, and leadership. These traits make them true role models.

They inspire us to be better in our own lives. They remind us that greatness is within reach for anyone willing to work for it. As we move forward, we can carry these lessons with us. They will guide us in whatever path we choose to follow. And now, let's explore the modern icons who continue to shape the game today.

CHAPTER 4
MODERN DAY ICONS

4.1 PATRICK MAHOMES: THE RISE OF A SUPERSTAR

Patrick Mahomes is a modern day NFL icon whose journey began long before he ever set foot on a professional field. Born in Tyler, Texas, Mahomes didn't just fall into greatness. He worked for it. During his time at Texas Tech University, he dazzled with his ability to throw the ball over 5,000 yards and score over 50 touchdowns in a single college season. This incredible performance caught the attention of NFL scouts, leading to his selection by the Kansas City Chiefs as the 10th overall pick in the 2017 NFL Draft.

Mahomes' rise was nothing short of meteoric. After the Chiefs traded their starting quarterback, he got his chance to shine in 2018. From his first season, he showed he was no ordinary player. Mahomes became known for his unique playing style. He could throw the ball in ways no one had seen before. Sometimes he tossed it sidearm, other times with his left hand. His ability to move quickly and escape defenders made him a constant threat on the field. Mahomes seemed to have a sixth sense, knowing exactly when to run and when to pass. His quick thinking and sharp instincts allowed him to make decisions in the blink of an eye, keeping defenses guessing and fans on the edge of their seats.

Mahomes didn't just play the game. He transformed it. In his first full season as a starter, he threw for over 5,000 yards and 50 touchdowns, joining the ranks of legends. He became the youngest quarterback to be named NFL MVP. His list of achievements kept growing. Mahomes led the Chiefs to a Super Bowl victory in 2020, earning the Super Bowl MVP title. He broke records, becoming the fastest quarterback to reach 10,000 passing yards. Every time he stepped onto the field, Mahomes set a new standard for what a quarterback could be. His multiple Pro Bowl selections proved he was among the best of the best.

His influence extends beyond his own performances. Mahomes has changed how people view the quarterback position. His success shows that you don't need to follow a script to be great. Young players now try to mimic his style. They practice throwing on the run and making quick decisions. Mahomes' impact reaches into youth football. Camps and programs teach kids his techniques, encouraging them to play with creativity and confidence. He's inspiring a new generation to dream big and redefine what's possible on the field. The way Mahomes plays has shifted expectations, showing that with talent and hard work, the sky's the limit for any aspiring athlete.

Reflection: What Makes Mahomes Special?

Consider what sets Patrick Mahomes apart. Think about his skills, achievements, and influence. Write down a few reasons why Mahomes is a modern icon in football. How does his story inspire you in your own life? Discuss with a friend and share your thoughts.

4.2 AARON DONALD: POWER AND PRECISION

When you think of a powerful and precise force on the football field, Aaron Donald comes to mind. He plays as a defensive tackle, one of the most challenging positions. Picture him standing strong on the defensive line, ready to face any opponent. Donald combines quickness with incredible strength, making him a nightmare for offensive players. He moves with the speed of a much smaller player, yet his strength is unmatched. This blend allows him to tackle running backs and rush the quarterback with ease. His versatility is key. Whether he's stopping a run or chasing down a passer, Donald's skills keep offenses on their toes.

Donald's career is filled with impressive highlights and awards. He has won the NFL Defensive Player of the Year award twice. This honor shows just how important he is to his team and the league. Every year, he earns a spot on the All-Pro team, marking him as one of the best players in his position. His trophy shelf is packed, but his impact goes beyond awards. Donald changes games with his presence. Coaches plan special strategies just to deal with him. His ability to disrupt plays is something special. Fans of all ages watch in awe as he breaks through lines and makes big tackles.

To stay at the top, Donald follows a strict training and preparation routine. He spends hours in the gym, working on every muscle. His workouts are intense, focusing on building strength and agility. He lifts heavy weights, runs sprints, and practices drills that improve his speed and balance. But it's not just about physical training. Donald also focuses on his diet. He eats meals that give him energy and help his body recover. This includes lots of protein, healthy fats, and the right amount of carbs. Mental preparation is just as important. Donald studies his opponents carefully. He watches game tapes to understand their weaknesses. This helps him anticipate their moves and stay one step ahead during games.

Donald's role extends beyond his physical abilities. He serves as a mentor and leader in the Los Angeles Rams locker room. Younger players look up to him, learning from his work ethic and dedication. He encourages them to push their limits and strive for greatness. Donald's voice carries weight. When he speaks, his teammates listen. He knows how to motivate others, sharing tips and advice that help them improve. His leadership helps create a positive team culture. He inspires those around him to give their best effort, fostering a sense of unity and purpose.

Being a leader isn't just about what happens on the field. It's about character and how you treat others. Donald understands this well. He leads by example, showing respect and sportsmanship at all times. His teammates admire his commitment to the game and to them. They know they can count on him, both in tough games and in practice. Donald's influence spreads through the team, building trust and camaraderie. His presence makes everyone better. When the Rams take the field, you can feel the energy and confidence he brings. It's contagious, lifting the team to new heights.

4.3 RUSSELL WILSON: LEADERSHIP AND LEGACY

Russell Wilson's path to NFL stardom is one of grit and overcoming the odds. Standing at 5'11", he faced doubts about his height, as many believed quarterbacks needed to be taller to succeed. Yet, Wilson didn't let this hold him back. He worked tirelessly to prove that skill and heart matter more than height. He played college football at North Carolina State and later the University of Wisconsin, where he led his team to a Big Ten title. His determination paid off when the Seattle Seahawks selected him in the third round of the 2012 NFL Draft. Many teams had overlooked him, but the Seahawks saw his potential. In his rookie year, he quickly became a star, leading the team to the playoffs and showing everyone that he belonged in the league.

Wilson's leadership goes beyond his impressive stats. On the field, he guides the Seahawks with calm and confidence. He makes smart decisions, especially when the pressure is on. His poise in critical moments has led to many thrilling victories. Under his leadership, the Seahawks have made multiple playoff appearances. He led them to a memorable win in Super Bowl XLVIII, where they defeated the Denver Broncos. His ability to stay focused and lead his team through tough games sets him apart. Wilson's teammates trust him, knowing he will give his all to help them succeed. He lifts those around him, making everyone play at their best.

Wilson's achievements and contributions to the game are significant. He has been selected for the Pro Bowl several times, an honor that recognizes the best players in the league. His style of play, combining passing with the ability to run when needed, has made him a versatile threat. Defenses struggle to contain him, as he can change the game with a single play. Wilson's knack for turning plays into positive gains has made him one of the most exciting quarterbacks to watch. His work ethic and dedication have earned him respect from fans and fellow players alike. His impact on the field is undeniable.

Beyond football, Wilson makes a difference in the community. He founded the Why Not You Foundation, which focuses on education and youth empowerment. Through this foundation, he supports schools and programs that encourage young people to dream big. Wilson regularly visits hospitals, lifting the spirits of sick children. His kindness and generosity inspire those around him. He also engages in speaking events, where he shares his story and encourages others to chase their dreams. Wilson's commitment to giving back shows that he understands the power of his influence. He uses it to make the world a better place, one act of kindness at a time.

Wilson's legacy is built on more than just his football skills. It's about how he lives his life and the positive impact he has on others. His story teaches us that you can overcome any challenge with hard work and determination. By staying true to yourself and never giving up, you can achieve great things. Wilson shows that leadership isn't just about leading a team to victory. It's about inspiring others and making a lasting difference in the world. His journey reminds us that no dream is too big and no challenge is too great if you believe in yourself and work hard.

4.4 OFF THE FIELD: COMMUNITY HEROES

Beyond their incredible skills on the field, many players shine brightly as community heroes. They use their fame to make a real difference in the world. These players know that their influence goes far beyond scoring touchdowns or making tackles. They take on the responsibility of using their voices and resources to create positive change. By addressing important issues like social justice and equality, they help raise awareness and drive action. They support education and youth development programs, knowing that young people are the future. Their efforts show that being a hero isn't just about what you do in the game. It's about how you impact lives outside of it.

Patrick Mahomes, Russell Wilson, and Aaron Donald are standout examples of players who have made significant contributions off the field. Mahomes founded the 15 and the Mahomies Foundation. This organization focuses on improving the lives of children through programs that emphasize health, wellness, and education. Mahomes is involved in various charitable activities, from funding local community projects to supporting schools. He shows that helping others can be a powerful part of one's legacy. Meanwhile, Russell Wilson regularly visits hospitals, bringing smiles and hope to children facing tough battles. His visits make a big impact, not just for the kids, but for their families too. His kindness and positive energy remind everyone of the importance of caring for others.

Aaron Donald also uses his platform for good. He works with underprivileged communities, offering support and resources to those who need it most. Donald understands the challenges many face, and he strives to make a difference. His efforts include hosting events and providing supplies to help families in need. By doing this, he shows that it's possible to lead with both strength and heart. These examples of community engagement highlight how players can use their status for meaningful causes. They prove that true leadership involves giving back and making a lasting impact on others.

Giving back is a central part of being a community leader. NFL players like Mahomes, Wilson, and Donald encourage young fans to get involved in their own communities. They inspire kids to think about how they can help others, whether it's volunteering or starting a small project. By sharing stories of lives changed through their initiatives, these players motivate fans to take action. They show that even small acts of kindness can have a big ripple effect. Their stories inspire other athletes to step up as well, fostering a culture of responsibility and empathy.

The broader impact of their efforts is profound. These players set an example that goes beyond football. They inspire young athletes to pursue leadership roles, on and off the field. Kids see their favorite stars making a difference and realize they can do the same. This influence helps cultivate a generation that values giving back and helping others. The actions of these players encourage a sense of community, showing that everyone can play a part in creating a better world. Their dedication to positive change inspires peers and fans alike to follow in their footsteps.

By using their talents and resources to address important issues, these modern icons exemplify what it means to be heroes. Their commitment to social justice, education, and youth development serves as a powerful reminder that the impact of an athlete goes far beyond the game. As we move forward, the stories of these community heroes inspire us to reflect on how we can make a difference, no matter our own circumstances. Their legacy is not just about winning games, but about winning hearts and minds, encouraging all of us to contribute positively to our world.

CHAPTER 5
GIANTS OF THE GAME

5.1 WILLIAM "REFRIGERATOR" PERRY: DOMINANCE ON THE DEFENSIVE LINE

Have you ever seen a player so big that he seems like a wall on the field? Meet William "Refrigerator" Perry, a giant in the world of football. Perry earned his nickname because of his massive size. He was as big and strong as a refrigerator. Standing at 6 feet 2 inches and weighing over 330 pounds, he was a force to be reckoned with. Perry played as a defensive tackle, and his presence was felt by everyone on the field. His size and strength made it hard for opponents to move him. He became famous for his role with the Chicago Bears, a team he helped lead to victory in Super Bowl XX.

Perry's journey to the NFL began at Clemson University, where he played college football. At Clemson, he was a star player, known for his incredible strength and skill. He helped his team win the national championship in 1981. In 1984, he was named the ACC Player of the Year. Coaches and players admired his ability to dominate the field. When the Chicago Bears drafted him in the first round of the 1985 NFL Draft, fans were excited to see what he could do. Perry quickly became a key player for the Bears, using his size to his advantage. His ability to block and tackle made him a valuable asset to the team. He was not just a player; he was a game-changer.

Perry's size gave him a unique style of play. On the defensive line, he used his long reach to grab and push opponents. This made it difficult for them to advance the ball. His blocking abilities set him apart. Perry could stop players in their tracks, disrupting their plays. His mere presence intimidated opponents. They knew they had to work hard to get past him. Perry's ability to fill gaps and control the line of scrimmage was unmatched. He played with a combination of power and finesse, making him a standout in every game.

To maintain his size and agility, Perry followed a strict training regimen. He spent a lot of time in the weight room, lifting heavy weights to build and keep his strength. His workouts included exercises that improved his agility, allowing him to move quickly despite his size. Conditioning routines ensured he stayed fit and ready to play. Perry's dedication to training showed in his performance. He could move with surprising speed, catching opponents off guard. His work ethic became an example for other players to follow. Perry's approach to fitness and training was a big part of his success on the field.

Perry's influence in the NFL was significant. He changed how teams viewed the role of a defensive tackle. His performance in key games showed that size and skill could dominate the field. In Super Bowl XX, Perry scored a touchdown as a fullback, showcasing his versatility. This moment became iconic, highlighting his unique abilities. Coaches began to see the value of players with both size and agility. Perry's presence on the defensive line forced teams to rethink their strategies. His impact went beyond his own team, influencing the game on a larger scale.

Reflection: The Power of Presence

Think about how William "Refrigerator" Perry used his size to change the game. How did his presence on the field impact his team and opponents? Write down your thoughts or share them with a friend. Consider how you can use your own unique qualities to make a difference, whether in sports, school, or everyday life.

5.2 ROB GRONKOWSKI: THE UNSTOPPABLE TIGHT END

Rob Gronkowski, often known simply as "Gronk," is one of the most famous tight ends to play in the NFL. His path to stardom began at the University of Arizona, where he quickly made a name for himself with his exceptional play. Gronkowski dominated the field with his size and skill, becoming a star player for the Wildcats. Even in college, his ability to catch passes and block defenders set him apart. Scouts noticed his talent and potential, which led to his selection in the 2010 NFL Draft. The New England Patriots picked him in the second round, and this marked the start of an incredible professional career. Joining the Patriots was a perfect fit for Gronkowski. He quickly became a key player on the team, known for his big plays and touchdowns.

What makes Gronkowski truly special is his physical presence on the field. Standing at 6'6" and weighing around 265 pounds, he uses his size to his advantage. Defenders struggle to match his strength and reach, making him a difficult target to cover. When the ball is in the air, Gronkowski can overpower defenders to make contested catches. His physicality also shines in blocking. In running plays, he uses his size to push defenders away, creating space for his teammates. This combination of skills makes him a versatile and valuable player. Gronkowski's ability to contribute in both the passing and running game sets him apart from many other tight ends. His presence on the field changes the dynamic of the game, giving his team an edge.

Throughout his career, Gronkowski has achieved many milestones. He has won multiple Super Bowls with the New England Patriots and the Tampa Bay Buccaneers. His performances in these games were crucial for his teams' victories. Gronkowski's ability to rise to the occasion during important matches earned him a reputation as a clutch player. He has been selected for the Pro Bowl several times, which recognizes him as one of the best in his position. His career stats are impressive, with numerous touchdowns and receiving yards to his name. Each season, Gronkowski shows why he is considered one of the greatest tight ends in NFL history.

Beyond his on-field achievements, Gronkowski is known for his charismatic personality. Fans love his fun and energetic nature. He often appears in media, sharing his enthusiasm for life and the game. Gronkowski's sense of humor and genuine character make him relatable and likable. Off the field, he engages in community work and charity events. He supports causes that help young athletes and children in need. Through his Gronk Nation Youth Foundation, he promotes sports and education. Gronkowski's positive influence extends beyond football, making him a role model for young fans. He shows that it's possible to be successful and still have fun while giving back to the community.

5.3 VINCE WILFORK: THE WALL OF DEFENSE

Picture a massive wall that seems impossible to break through. That's Vince Wilfork on the football field. As a defensive tackle, he played a crucial role in stopping the run game. Imagine trying to run the football through a brick wall. That's what it felt like for many players facing Wilfork. He clogged up the middle of the field with his size and strength. Offensive linemen struggled to move him, which made it hard for running backs to find any open space. His presence was intimidating. He could read plays quickly and react with precision. When runners tried to slip by, Wilfork used his quick hands and swift movements to bring them down. He knew how to position himself perfectly, making it nearly impossible for the offense to gain yards on the ground. By plugging gaps and holding his ground, he created opportunities for his teammates to make big plays.

Wilfork's career was full of achievements that speak to his skill and impact on the game. He won two Super Bowl titles with the New England Patriots, contributing to their success with his powerful play. His efforts on the field earned him several All-Pro selections, recognizing him as one of the best defensive tackles in the league. Wilfork was a key player in the Patriots' strong defensive line, known for his ability to disrupt plays and frustrate quarterbacks. Beyond the statistics, his leadership and presence inspired those around him. He was a player that every offense had to plan for, knowing he could change the course of a game with his ability to stop the run and pressure the quarterback. His contributions were vital to the team's victories and defensive strategies.

To maintain his strength and agility, Wilfork paid close attention to his training and conditioning. He focused on building strength through weightlifting, spending hours in the gym to keep his muscles strong and powerful. But it wasn't just about lifting weights. Wilfork understood the importance of endurance training, which helped him stay active and effective throughout games. He worked on his stamina with various drills, ensuring he could perform at his best from the first play to the last. His dedication to fitness was evident in his performance. Despite his size, Wilfork moved with surprising speed and agility, making it difficult for opponents to predict his actions. His training routine allowed him to maintain his role as a dominant force on the field, showcasing his commitment to excellence.

Wilfork's influence extended beyond his physical abilities. He was a natural leader, both on and off the field. Younger players looked up to him, learning from his experience and dedication. He took the time to mentor them, offering guidance and advice that helped them grow into better athletes. Wilfork led by example, showing that hard work and perseverance could lead to success. His leadership created a sense of unity among his teammates. Off the field, Wilfork was active in community service, using his platform to give back. He participated in various initiatives to support those in need, demonstrating the importance of using one's influence for good. His commitment to helping others highlighted the impact a player can have beyond the game, leaving a lasting impression on the community and the league.

5.4 SIZE AND SKILL: BALANCING POWER WITH AGILITY

In the world of football, size is a huge advantage. But without agility, even the biggest players can struggle. Balancing power with quickness is critical. Imagine a giant on the field. They can block and push, but if they can't move quickly, they become an easy target. That's why agility drills are so important. Players use these drills to improve their speed and change direction fast. They work on their footwork, making sure they can pivot and sprint without losing balance. Flexibility training also plays a big role. Stretching helps muscles stay loose, preventing injuries and allowing for wider ranges of movement. This balance of size and agility keeps players competitive and effective.

To enhance agility, larger players often use plyometrics and speed training. Plyometrics includes exercises like jump squats and box jumps. These movements build explosive power and help athletes react quickly. Speed training involves sprints and shuttle runs. It focuses on quick bursts of movement. Both methods increase a player's ability to move swiftly despite their size. Many players also incorporate yoga and Pilates into their routines. These practices improve flexibility and core strength. They help players maintain control over their movements, even when they're pushed around. By blending these techniques, players create a powerful and agile game style.

Training for big players has come a long way. In the past, the focus was mainly on gaining strength. Now, training includes a wide range of activities. Nutrition plays a key role in this evolution. Players follow diets that fuel their bodies and boost recovery. They eat foods rich in protein, healthy fats, and carbs. This helps them stay strong and energetic. Recovery techniques have also advanced. Ice baths, massages, and stretching help muscles heal after intense workouts. These methods ensure that players remain in top condition, ready for every game. By focusing on overall fitness, larger players can perform at high levels, combining strength with speed and skill.

Teams use the size of their players strategically. Larger players are often placed in specific formations and play designs. On offense, they might serve as blockers, opening paths for runners. On defense, they might form the first line of resistance, stopping opponents in their tracks. Coaches design plays that leverage the strengths of their biggest players. They create matchups that favor size and power, using them to control the game's pace. This strategic use of size can change the flow of a match. It forces opponents to adjust and find new tactics. The impact of size on strategy highlights the importance of having players who can move well and use their size to their advantage.

As we move forward, the balance of size and skill becomes more important in football. Players who master this balance can dominate the field. They can outmaneuver opponents and create opportunities for their teams. The strategies and training methods we see today continue to evolve. They help players become more versatile and effective. In the next chapter, we'll explore how defensive players use their skills to stop even the most powerful offenses, showcasing the art of smart and strategic play.

CHAPTER 6
DEFENSIVE DYNAMOS

6.1 THE STEEL CURTAIN: PITTSBURGH'S LEGENDARY LINE

A pack of unstoppable warriors is charging forward with unmatched power and precision. They form a barrier that offenses fear to face. This was the Steel Curtain, the legendary defense of the Pittsburgh Steelers from the 1970s. Known for their fierce determination and incredible skill, this group of players changed the way football was played. The Steel Curtain wasn't just a nickname; it was a symbol of strength and resilience that struck fear into the hearts of opponents. Imagine trying to get past a wall made of steel, and you'll understand why this defense was so respected and admired.

The formation of the Steel Curtain was no accident. It came together piece by piece, built by players who were each remarkable in their own way. Joe Greene, often called "Mean Joe," was the heart of this defense. His intensity and leadership set the tone. L.C. Greenwood brought speed and agility, using his long arms to block passes and disrupt plays. Ernie Holmes, with his raw power, could bulldoze through offensive lines. Dwight White, nicknamed "Mad Dog," played with relentless energy. Together, they formed a unit that was nearly impossible to beat. Behind these players stood Bud Carson, the defensive coordinator. He crafted the strategies that made the Steel Curtain so effective. Carson's plans allowed these players to use their strengths to the fullest.

The Steel Curtain influenced defensive strategies across the entire league. They pioneered aggressive pass rush techniques, constantly pressuring quarterbacks and forcing mistakes. Their style of play showed other teams the value of a strong and coordinated defense. Teams began to copy their methods, hoping to capture some of the Steel Curtain's magic. The Steelers' defense wasn't just about stopping the run or blocking passes. They created chaos on the field, confusing offenses and taking control of games. Their ability to read plays and react quickly made them a force to be reckoned with. As a result, they became the model for future defenses, changing how coaches approached the defensive side of the game.

The success of the Steel Curtain is measured not just in victories but in the legacy they left behind. During the 1970s, the Steelers won four Super Bowls, a testament to the strength of their defense. They didn't just win games; they dominated them. In the 1976 season, the Steel Curtain recorded five shutouts, allowing only 3.1 points per game after losing star quarterback Terry Bradshaw to injury. This impressive feat highlighted their ability to carry the team, even when the offense struggled. Eight of their starting eleven defensive players were selected for the Pro Bowl in 1976, with four eventually making it to the Hall of Fame. Their contributions to the team's success cemented their place in football history.

But the Steel Curtain was more than just a group of talented players. They became a symbol of Pittsburgh's blue-collar identity. The city, known for its steel production, embraced this defense as a reflection of its hardworking spirit. The nickname "Steel Curtain" was coined by a ninth grader from Pittsburgh in a radio contest, capturing the essence of both the team and the city. Fans took pride in their team's grit and determination, and the Steel Curtain's success brought the community together. On game days, the city buzzed with excitement, and the Steelers' victories became a source of local pride. The Steel Curtain's impact went beyond the field, strengthening Pittsburgh's community spirit and leaving a lasting legacy that continues to inspire fans today.

Reflection: Building Your Own "Steel Curtain"

Think about what it takes to build a strong team, just like the Steel Curtain. What qualities do you need? How can you work together to achieve your goals? Write down some ideas or discuss with friends. Consider how teamwork and determination can help you succeed in whatever you choose to do.

6.2 RAY LEWIS: HEART OF A LINEBACKER

Envision stepping onto a football field, surrounded by the roar of cheering fans. The air buzzes with energy, and you feel the weight of the game on your shoulders. This is where Ray Lewis found his calling. Drafted by the Baltimore Ravens in 1996, Lewis quickly became one of the most feared linebackers in the NFL. From the start, he showed extraordinary skill and a natural talent for the game. In his rookie year, he earned the Defensive Rookie of the Year title. This early recognition was just the beginning of a career filled with highlights and achievements. Lewis became known for his fierce tackling and incredible ability to read plays before they happened. He was always in the right place at the right time, making game-changing plays that left opponents in awe.

Lewis's defensive skills were unmatched, setting him apart as an exceptional linebacker. He had a knack for tackling that seemed almost instinctual. His quick reactions and relentless pursuit made him a nightmare for offenses. He could bring down the toughest players with ease, using both strength and technique. But Lewis wasn't just about physical prowess. He was a strategic thinker, always analyzing the game and anticipating the opponent's next move. His intensity was palpable, both on the field and in the locker room. Lewis led by example, pushing his teammates to give their best. His presence inspired those around him to rise to his level, creating a culture of excellence and dedication within the Ravens.

Throughout his career, Lewis achieved numerous milestones that solidified his place in football history. He was named NFL Defensive Player of the Year twice, a testament to his impact on the game. In Super Bowl XXXV, Lewis's performance was nothing short of spectacular, earning him the title of Super Bowl MVP. His leadership and skill helped the Ravens claim victory, showing the world what made him a true champion. Lewis's career stats are impressive, with countless tackles and key plays that changed the course of games. His ability to dominate on defense earned him respect from players and fans alike. These achievements reflect not only his talent but also his work ethic and determination to succeed.

Lewis's influence went beyond his physical abilities. His leadership was a powerful force, motivating his team and inspiring fans. Before each game, he delivered passionate speeches that fired up his teammates. His words resonated deeply, instilling a sense of purpose and unity. Lewis had a unique ability to connect with others, lifting their spirits and encouraging them to push through challenges. His motivational presence became a cornerstone of the Ravens' identity, shaping the team's culture and approach to the game. Fans admired his dedication and charisma, drawing inspiration from his journey and achievements. Lewis showed that true leadership involves both heart and strength, on and off the field.

The Ravens' defense reflected Lewis's spirit and tenacity. He influenced the team's strategy and mindset, emphasizing the importance of resilience and teamwork. His dedication to the game inspired those around him to strive for greatness, creating a legacy that continues to impact the Ravens today. Lewis's story is one of perseverance and passion, demonstrating that with hard work and belief, anything is possible. As fans watched him play, they saw more than just a great linebacker. They saw a leader who brought out the best in everyone around him. Lewis's journey remains a powerful reminder of the impact one person can have on a team, and the lasting legacy they can leave behind.

6.3 DEION SANDERS: SPEED AND SWAGGER

Imagine being so fast that when you run, it feels like you're flying. This is the kind of speed Deion Sanders had. But that's not all that made him special. Sanders wasn't just a great football player. He also played professional baseball. It's rare for someone to excel in two sports at such a high level, but Sanders did just that. In football, he played for teams like the Atlanta Falcons, San Francisco 49ers, and Dallas Cowboys. In baseball, he spent time with the New York Yankees and Atlanta Braves. This dual-sport career made him one of the most unique athletes of his time.

On the football field, Sanders was known for his outstanding defensive skills. He played the position of cornerback, where his main job was to stop wide receivers from catching the ball. Sanders had a knack for this. His speed allowed him to keep up with the fastest players. He could change direction quickly, making it hard for opponents to get away. But it wasn't just his physical skills that set him apart. Sanders had a certain style and confidence that made him stand out. He played with swagger, a kind of cool confidence that said he was in control. His presence on the field was electrifying. He was a true shutdown cornerback, someone quarterbacks tried to avoid because of his ability to intercept passes and change the game.

Sanders' career is filled with achievements that highlight his greatness. He won two Super Bowl titles, showcasing his talent on the biggest stages. His contributions to the game were recognized when he was inducted into the Pro Football Hall of Fame. These accomplishments speak to his skill and dedication. Sanders didn't just play the game; he mastered it. His ability to perform under pressure and deliver when it mattered most made him a legend. But his influence went beyond the field. Sanders became a cultural icon, known for his "Prime Time" persona. This was more than just a nickname. It was a way of life that captured his flair and charisma. He knew how to entertain, both on and off the field. Whether it was dancing after a big play or speaking with the media, Sanders always had the spotlight.

Beyond sports, Sanders made a significant impact on popular culture. He appeared in commercials, TV shows, and movies, further cementing his status as a household name. Sanders used his platform to reach people in new ways, sharing his love for sports and life with a broader audience. His contributions to sports broadcasting and entertainment brought a new level of excitement to the game. He showed that athletes could be more than just players; they could be entertainers and role models too. Sanders' influence extended to fashion as well. His style, both on and off the field, inspired many. He was never afraid to be bold and different, encouraging others to be true to themselves.

Sanders' career and impact remind us that sports can be a way to connect and inspire. His speed and swagger set a new standard for what it means to be a great athlete. He taught us that with confidence and hard work, you can achieve incredible things. Sanders' story continues to inspire young athletes to dream big and pursue their passions with the same energy and enthusiasm that he brought to everything he did.

6.4 DEFENSIVE PLAYBOOKS: STRATEGIES FOR SUCCESS

When you think of football, you might picture the fast-moving action on the field. But behind every great play, there's a carefully crafted strategy. Defenses use different formations to stop the offense from scoring. Two of the most common are the "3-4 defense" and the "4-3 defense." In the "3-4 defense," there are three defensive linemen and four linebackers. This setup offers flexibility, allowing the defense to disguise their intentions. The extra linebacker can either rush the passer or drop back into coverage. On the other hand, the "4-3 defense" uses four linemen and three linebackers. This formation is strong against the run, as the four linemen can control the line of scrimmage. It provides a straightforward approach, focusing on stopping the opposing team's running game. Each formation has its strengths, and coaches choose them based on the opponent's style of play.

Beyond these basic setups, defenses also use specialized packages like the "Nickel" and "Dime." These packages are designed for situations where the offense is likely to pass the ball. In a "Nickel" package, a fifth defensive back is added to the formation. This helps cover additional receivers and provides more speed on the field. The "Dime" package takes this even further by adding a sixth defensive back. This is useful against teams that rely heavily on passing. These packages allow defenses to adapt to different offensive strategies. They ensure that the defense can match the speed and agility of the offense, making it harder for the quarterback to find open receivers.

Defensive tactics and techniques are key to countering offensive plays. One such tactic is blitzing. This involves sending extra players to rush the quarterback, often catching the offense by surprise. Blitzing can force hurried throws or lead to sacks, disrupting the offense's rhythm. However, it's risky because it leaves fewer defenders in coverage. Another common strategy is zone coverage. Instead of covering a specific player, defenders cover an area of the field. This strategy allows defenders to watch the quarterback's eyes and react to the ball. Zone coverage can be effective against teams with strong passing attacks, as it creates opportunities for interceptions.

Defensive lines use stunts and twists to confuse offensive linemen. A stunt involves two or more linemen switching places after the snap. This can create gaps in the offensive line, allowing a defender to get to the quarterback. Twists are similar, but involve more complex movements. These techniques require precise timing and coordination. When executed well, they can disrupt the offensive line's protection and lead to big plays for the defense. Coaches use these tactics to keep the offense guessing, forcing them to adjust their blocking schemes on the fly.

The defensive coordinator is the mastermind behind these strategies. Their job is to analyze opponent tendencies and weaknesses. They study game film, looking for patterns in the offense's play-calling. By understanding how the opposing team operates, the coordinator can craft a game plan that exploits their weaknesses. This may involve focusing on stopping a star player or adjusting formations to counter specific plays. The coordinator's ability to adapt and plan is crucial to a defense's success. A well-prepared defense can change the course of a game, shutting down even the most potent offenses.

Some defensive strategies have become legendary for their innovation. One example is Bill Belichick's game plan against the St. Louis Rams, known as the "Greatest Show on Turf." In Super Bowl XXXVI, Belichick's New England Patriots focused on disrupting the Rams' timing and rhythm. By being physical with receivers and pressuring the quarterback, they held the Rams to just 17 points, leading to a Patriots victory. Another iconic strategy is the Seattle Seahawks' "Legion of Boom." This defense was known for its aggressive play and hard-hitting style. They excelled in creating turnovers and limiting big plays, helping the Seahawks win Super Bowl XLVIII.

Defenses are the backbone of a successful team. Their strategies and tactics shape the game, creating opportunities to win. As we move forward, we'll see how these defensive principles apply to modern-day icons who continue to elevate the game.

CHAPTER 7
OFFENSIVE
POWERHOUSES

7.1 PEYTON MANNING: THE MASTERMIND QUARTERBACK

Peyton Manning wasn't just a player; he was a strategist. Manning's journey to becoming one of the most respected quarterbacks began long before he took the NFL by storm. At the University of Tennessee, he showed promise with his sharp mind and strong arm. Manning led the Volunteers to several victories, setting records for passing yards and touchdowns. Coaches and fans admired his leadership and ability to read defenses. His college success made him a top prospect in the 1998 NFL Draft, where the Indianapolis Colts chose him as the first overall pick.

Manning's rise to greatness wasn't just about talent. It was about preparation. He studied his opponents like a detective solving a mystery. Manning spent countless hours watching game tapes, analyzing every detail. He learned the tendencies of defenses, understanding how they moved and reacted. Before each play, he performed detailed pre-snap reads, observing the defense's setup. Manning then used audibles—changes in play calls made on the spot—to adjust his strategy. This approach allowed him to exploit weaknesses and take advantage of opportunities. His preparation set a new standard for quarterbacks and changed how the position was played.

Throughout his career, Manning achieved milestones that few could imagine. He won two Super Bowl titles, leading his teams to victory with skill and poise. Manning was named NFL MVP five times, more than any other player in history. In 2013, he broke the record for the most touchdown passes in a single season, throwing an astounding 55 touchdowns. These accomplishments speak to his hard work and dedication. Manning's success on the field made him a legend, admired by fans and players alike. His ability to perform under pressure and lead his team to victory was unmatched.

Manning's influence extended beyond his own achievements. He changed the way quarterbacks approached the game. His use of the no-huddle offense, where the team quickly lines up for the next play without a huddle, became a key strategy. This kept defenses off balance and allowed for faster-paced games.

Manning's style encouraged quarterbacks to think on their feet and adapt quickly. He also shared his knowledge through football camps, mentoring young quarterbacks. Manning taught them the importance of preparation and the value of studying the game. His impact on the sport continues, inspiring the next generation of players to follow his example.

Interactive Element: Create Your Own Play

Think like Peyton Manning and draw up your own football play! Use a piece of paper to sketch the positions of your teammates. Decide if your play will be a run or a pass. Use arrows to show the movement of players. Once you've drawn your play, explain it to a friend or family member. Discuss how you would execute it in a game. This exercise helps you understand the planning and strategy that go into each play, just like Manning did on the field.

7.2 BARRY SANDERS: ELUSIVE RUNNING BACK

Dodging defenders with just a quick twist of the body is what Barry Sanders did almost every time he touched the ball. His playing style was all about agility and elusiveness. Sanders had a unique ability to make defenders miss him. He used signature moves like the spin and juke to slip through even the tightest defenses. Picture him running full speed, then suddenly changing direction in a flash. Defenders would dive, only to grab air as Sanders accelerated past them. His feet moved so quickly, it looked like he was dancing over the field. This combination of speed and agility made him a nightmare for defenses.

Throughout his career, Barry Sanders achieved incredible success. He played in the NFL for ten seasons, becoming a ten-time Pro Bowl selection. This honor showed he was one of the best players in the league year after year. In 1997, he won the NFL MVP award, highlighting his impact on the game. Sanders rushed for over 15,000 yards in his career, an achievement that places him among the greatest running backs in history. His ability to gain yards and score touchdowns made him a constant threat on the field. Fans loved watching him play, knowing he could turn any play into a highlight reel.

Despite his success, Sanders chose to retire early. This decision shocked many fans and experts. He was still at the top of his game, but Sanders wanted to leave football on his own terms. He valued his health and personal happiness more than breaking records. His retirement impacted the Detroit Lions, the team he played for. Losing such a talented player was a big blow. The NFL also felt his absence. Sanders brought excitement to every game, and his unexpected leave left a void in the sport. Yet, his choice to step away on his own terms showed strength and independence, inspiring others to prioritize what matters most to them.

Barry Sanders's legacy continues to inspire running backs today. Players study his moves, hoping to learn from the master of elusiveness. His ability to change direction and avoid tackles is something many young athletes try to replicate. Sanders's influence can be seen in the new generation of runners who use agility and speed to outsmart defenses. Even after retiring, Sanders remains active in the football community. He participates in charity work, using his platform to give back. His presence in the community shows that his impact goes beyond the field. Sanders's story inspires young players to dream big and stay true to themselves, both in sports and in life.

7.3 RANDY MOSS: CATCHING GREATNESS

Randy Moss played with a combination of speed and power that few could match. Moss was known for his ability to make deep-threat plays. This means he could catch long passes and score touchdowns from far away on the field. His leaping ability was incredible. He could jump high to grab passes that seemed out of reach. With his talent, he made difficult catches look easy. Moss had a natural gift for tracking the ball and adjusting his body to make the catch. Defenders found it incredibly hard to keep up with him or knock the ball away.

Randy Moss achieved many milestones in his career. In 1998, he was named the NFL Offensive Rookie of the Year. This award recognized him as one of the best new players in the league. Moss made a significant impact right from his first season. His most notable record came in 2007. That year, he caught 23 touchdown passes, the most ever in a single season. This achievement high-lighted his skill and consistency as a receiver. Over his career, Moss became known as one of the most prolific touchdown scorers in NFL history. His ability to find the end zone helped his teams to victory many times.

Defenses had to change how they played because of Moss. His speed and talent forced them to use double coverage often. This means two defenders would guard him instead of one. The strategy aimed to limit Moss's chances of catching the ball. However, even with extra attention, he still found ways to make big plays. Moss's influence went beyond just catching the ball. He changed how teams thought about defending against deep passes. The term "getting Mossed" became popular. It described the moments when Moss would out-jump or outplay defenders to make a spectacular catch.

Moss's playing style continues to inspire many of today's wide receivers. Young players watch his highlights, hoping to learn from his incredible skills. They see how he used speed and leaping to become a legend. Moss showed that receivers could be game-changers and not just support players. His influence on the field is still felt today. Beyond his playing days, Moss remains involved in football. He works as an analyst and commentator, sharing his knowledge of the game with fans. His insights help people understand the strategies and skills needed to succeed as a wide receiver. Moss's legacy lives on, teaching new generations of players what it takes to reach greatness.

7.4 OFFENSIVE MASTERY: PLAYS THAT CHANGED THE GAME

Think of a play so clever that it leaves everyone, even the toughest defenses, speechless. The "Philly Special" in Super Bowl LII is one such play. The Philadelphia Eagles faced a crucial moment against the New England Patriots. Instead of a regular play, they tried something bold. The quarterback, Nick Foles, moved to the side as if he wasn't involved. Suddenly, the ball was snapped to another player, who flipped it to a third player. Foles then caught a pass in the end zone for a touchdown. This trick play was both surprising and brilliant. It showed how creativity could change the course of a game. The "Philly Special" is now part of NFL lore, celebrated for its daring and execution.

Another legendary play is Joe Montana's "The Catch" to Dwight Clark in the 1981 NFC Championship Game. With the San Francisco 49ers trailing the Dallas Cowboys, Montana needed a miracle. He scrambled to his right, avoiding defenders. Then he threw the ball high into the end zone. Clark leaped into the air, reaching with his fingertips to make the catch. This play secured a victory and sent the 49ers to the Super Bowl. It was more than just a catch.

It was a moment that defined the team's rise to greatness. Fans still talk about it today, remembering the excitement and precision that made it possible.

These plays didn't just make headlines. They influenced how teams think about offense. The "Philly Special" highlighted the importance of unpredictability. Coaches saw the value in taking risks and trying new things. It encouraged other teams to develop their own trick plays, adding excitement and strategy to the game. Meanwhile, "The Catch" emphasized precision and timing. It showed the impact of perfect execution in critical moments. These iconic plays inspired coaches to focus on creativity and adaptability. They changed how games are played, making offense more dynamic and thrilling.

The introduction of the West Coast Offense was another game-changer. Developed by coach Bill Walsh, it focused on short, precise passes. This strategy aimed to control the ball and tire out defenses. It allowed teams to move the ball efficiently, even against strong opponents. The West Coast Offense became a blueprint for success, leading to many victories and championships. It taught teams the importance of timing and rhythm, influencing how offenses are structured today. This innovation paved the way for more advanced strategies, shaping the modern game.

Another significant development was the spread offense, which emerged in both college and professional football. This strategy spread players across the field, creating space and opportunities for big plays. It relied on quick passes and fast-paced action, challenging defenses to cover more ground. The spread offense became popular because it adapted well to different situations. It encouraged teams to use versatile players who could run, catch, and throw. This approach changed how offenses operated, emphasizing speed and flexibility.

Coaches played a critical role in these offensive evolutions. Bill Walsh's development of the West Coast Offense set a new standard for strategic thinking. His focus on precision and teamwork influenced countless coaches and players. Sean McVay, the head coach of the Los Angeles Rams, brought his own innovations. He used motion and misdirection to confuse defenses, keeping them guessing. McVay's approach highlighted the importance of adapting to changing game conditions. His success showed how modern coaching could blend creativity with discipline, inspiring others to push the boundaries of what's possible.

These iconic plays and strategies have also impacted player development. Young quarterbacks are now trained to read defenses quickly and make smart decisions. They learn to adapt and think on their feet, just like the pros. High school and college programs emphasize quarterback-read options, teaching players to analyze and react to defenses in real-time. This focus on preparation and quick thinking helps them succeed under pressure.

Wide receivers and running backs also benefit from these strategies. They develop versatile skill sets, learning to catch, run, and block. Coaches encourage them to be adaptable, ready to take on different roles based on the team's needs. This versatility makes them valuable assets, capable of contributing in various ways. As players embrace these lessons, they become better equipped to handle the demands of modern football.

In the end, offensive mastery is about more than just scoring points. It's about creativity, precision, and adaptability. These elements come together to create unforgettable moments and inspire future generations. As we look to the future, these lessons will continue to shape the game, driving innovation and excitement. Now, we turn our attention to the pioneers who paved the way for the NFL as we know it.

CHAPTER 8

HONORING THE
PIONEERS

8.1 VINCE LOMBARDI: THE MAN AND THE TROPHY

Think about a coach so inspiring that his name is on the trophy every NFL team dreams of winning. This coach was Vince Lombardi. Before he became a legend, Lombardi's journey began in Brooklyn, New York, in 1913. Growing up in a vibrant neighborhood, he developed a love for sports early on. After playing football himself, Lombardi's path to coaching started at Fordham University. Here, he was one of the "Seven Blocks of Granite," a name given to the tough players on the team. This experience taught him the value of teamwork and grit. After college, Lombardi took a coaching job at St. Cecilia High School. His time there showed his knack for inspiring young players. He later joined the U.S. Military Academy at West Point as an assistant coach. Here, he met Colonel Blaik, a mentor who shaped his coaching style. Blaik taught Lombardi the importance of discipline and precision. These lessons stayed with Lombardi and helped him build a coaching career full of success and respect.

Lombardi's career truly took off when he joined the Green Bay Packers in 1959. At the time, the Packers struggled to win games. But Lombardi believed in his team. He focused on teaching the basics and building a strong work ethic. His motto was simple: "Winning isn't everything, it's the only thing." This mindset pushed his players to give their best. Under Lombardi's leadership, the Packers became one of the most successful teams in NFL history. They won five NFL Championships in just seven years. Lombardi also guided them to victory in the first two Super Bowls. His teams were known for their skill and discipline. Players respected him because he pushed them hard but cared deeply about their success. Lombardi created a culture of winning and teamwork that few teams could match.

The Vince Lombardi Trophy is awarded every year to the Super Bowl champions. This trophy stands as a symbol of excellence and perseverance. It represents not just the victory but the hard work and dedication it takes to become the best. Lombardi's name on the trophy reminds teams of his values. It encourages them to strive for greatness with every game. The trophy's design is simple yet elegant, reflecting the straightforward but powerful approach Lombardi took in his coaching. Each year, when a team lifts the trophy, they honor Lombardi's legacy and the high standards he set for the sport.

Lombardi's impact on football goes beyond the trophies and titles. His principles continue to inspire coaches and players today. His famous speech, "What It Takes to Be Number One," talks about playing with heart and intelligence. He emphasized discipline and hard work, believing that these qualities led to true fulfillment. Lombardi's philosophies have shaped the way many coaches train their teams. They focus on fundamentals and building character. Even young players learn from his example. They see that success isn't just about talent. It's about using your skills wisely and working together as a team. Lombardi's influence stretches far beyond the field, making him a true pioneer in the world of sports.

Reflection: What Would Lombardi Do?

Imagine you're coaching a team for the first time. Think about the qualities Lombardi valued, like discipline, teamwork, and hard work. How would you use these to inspire your players? Write down your thoughts or discuss them with a friend. Consider how you can apply Lombardi's lessons to your own life, whether in sports, school, or any activity you love.

8.2 PAUL BROWN: INNOVATOR OF THE MODERN GAME

Paul Brown brought new ideas that transformed how teams played and practiced. One of his most important contributions was the introduction of the playbook. Before Brown, teams relied on players' memories to run plays. But Brown created detailed books that outlined every play. This helped players understand exactly what to do. It allowed for more complex strategies. Another innovation was the practice squad. Brown realized that having extra players to practice against would make the team better. These players helped the starters prepare for real games, improving their skills and readiness.

Brown also introduced film study as a regular part of team preparation. By watching films of past games, players could see their mistakes and learn from them. They could also study their opponents, figuring out their strengths and weaknesses. This approach gave Brown's teams a big edge. They went into games knowing exactly what to expect. It made them smarter and more strategic. Brown's focus on detailed game planning set a new standard in football. Coaches across the league began to adopt these methods, recognizing their value in creating well-prepared teams.

Beyond strategies, Brown changed how teams were organized. He established a hierarchical coaching staff. This means coaches had specific roles and responsibilities. It created a clear line of authority and communication. Each coach specialized in different areas, like defense or offense. This specialization made the team more efficient. Brown also focused on recruiting diverse talent pools. He looked for players with different skills and backgrounds. This diversity added depth and versatility to his teams. It allowed them to adapt to various challenges and opponents.

Brown achieved great success with the Cleveland Browns and later the Cincinnati Bengals. With the Browns, he dominated the All-America Football Conference (AAFC). His team won four championships in the AAFC's four years of existence. When the Browns joined the NFL, they continued to excel. They won three NFL titles under his leadership. Brown's influence extended to the founding of the Cincinnati Bengals. There, he shaped the team's early identity, building a foundation for future success. His ability to create winning teams showcased his genius as both a coach and a strategist.

Brown's legacy as a mentor and leader is profound. He guided many coaches who went on to achieve greatness themselves. Notable names include Bill Walsh and Don Shula. They learned from Brown's methods and adapted them to their own teams. Brown's influence can be seen in modern team-building and strategic operations. His focus on preparation, innovation, and teamwork continues to inspire coaches today. Young players and coaches look up to Brown's example. They see how his ideas transformed football and how they can apply similar principles to their own teams.

Interactive Element: Football Film Study

Try this: Watch a short video of a football game. Pay attention to what each player does on a play. Write down what you notice about their movements and decisions. Discuss with a friend or family member what worked well and what could be improved. This exercise helps you understand the benefits of film study, just like Paul Brown taught his teams. It shows how watching and learning can make you better, both on and off the field.

8.3 BILL WALSH: ARCHITECT OF THE WEST COAST OFFENSE

Before Bill Walsh became a legendary figure, he took on coaching roles at Stanford University and with the Cincinnati Bengals. At Stanford, he learned the importance of education and discipline, blending those with his love for football. His time at the Bengals was transformative. Here, he began to develop ideas that would change how teams played offense. Walsh believed in a system where passing was key, not just running the ball. While at the

Bengals, he started crafting strategies that focused on quick, accurate passes. This approach emphasized timing and skill over brute force. His ideas were a breath of fresh air in a league dominated by running plays. These concepts laid the groundwork for what would become known as the West Coast Offense.

The West Coast Offense was a game-changer. Imagine an offense that could move the ball with short, precise passes, keeping defenses guessing. That was Walsh's vision. This system didn't just rely on deep throws down the field. Instead, it used a series of short passes that spread the defense and opened up possibilities for longer gains. This approach required quarterbacks who could make quick decisions and receivers who knew their routes inside out. It was adaptable, allowing teams to adjust their play-calling based on what the defense showed them. Versatility was its strength. Defenses found it hard to predict, making it difficult to prepare against. This method of play allowed teams to control the pace of the game, keeping the defense on its heels and the offense in charge.

Walsh's success with the San Francisco 49ers cemented his reputation as an offensive genius. With the 49ers, he won three Super Bowls and built a dynasty. Under his leadership, the team became a powerhouse. Walsh's coaching helped develop Joe Montana, one of the greatest quarterbacks of all time. Montana thrived under the West Coast Offense, using quick passes to outsmart defenses. Walsh's system allowed Montana to shine, leading the 49ers to victory after victory. This partnership showcased the effectiveness of Walsh's strategies. They became the standard that many teams aimed to replicate. The 49ers' success under Walsh wasn't just about winning games. It was about changing how football was played and perceived.

Walsh's influence on coaching philosophy extends far beyond his time on the sidelines. His approach to the game encouraged creativity and innovation. Many teams adopted the West Coast Offense, recognizing its value in modern football. Coaches across the league began to see the benefits of Walsh's methods. They appreciated the focus on precision and timing. His legacy of problem-solving and thinking outside the box inspired a new generation of coaches. They began to explore new ideas and push the boundaries of traditional football strategies. Walsh's impact is still felt today, as teams continue to use his ideas to gain an edge over their opponents. His willingness to innovate paved the way for the diverse and dynamic offenses we see in the NFL now.

Bill Walsh not only changed the way a team plays but also left a lasting mark on the entire sport. His work wasn't just about creating a winning team. It was about transforming football into something more exciting and strategic. His ideas have become timeless, influencing how players are trained and how games are played. Coaches who learned from Walsh carry his teachings forward, ensuring his legacy lives on. The West Coast Offense remains a testament to Walsh's vision, reminding us of his contributions to the game.

8.4 PIONEERS' LEGACY: LESSONS FOR THE NEXT GENERATION

Pioneers looked at the game of football and saw endless possibilities. They weren't content with what was already there. They had visionary thinking and a willingness to try new things. They saw football not just as a game but as a canvas for strategy and teamwork. Their ideas weren't always popular at first. Yet, they pushed ahead, knowing that innovation was the key to progress. This dedication to excellence and continuous improvement defined their careers. They believed in always getting better, no matter how good they already were. This mindset allowed them to make lasting changes that shaped the sport.

Their impact on modern football is everywhere you look. Many of the strategies and systems they introduced are still in use today. Coaches study their methods, adapting them to fit the current game. The way teams organize practices, the plays they run, and even how they plan for opponents all have roots in these pioneers' ideas. This influence extends beyond just plays and strategies. It touches the very core of coaching styles and team management. Coaches who adopt these philosophies focus on building strong, cohesive teams. They emphasize preparation, discipline, and a deep understanding of the game.

These pioneers also played a big role in shaping NFL culture. They helped establish a competitive and dynamic environment. This is a place where every team aims to be the best. Their work promoted teamwork and sportsmanship, values that are central to football today. They understood that the game was not just about individual talent. It was about how well players worked together. This focus on collaboration created a sense of community within teams and among fans. It inspired a culture where respect and fair play are as important as winning.

Inspirational stories from these pioneers offer valuable lessons. One story tells of a coach who faced a losing streak but refused to give up. Instead of getting discouraged, he used this adversity to fuel his team's comeback. He taught his players to embrace change and adapt when things didn't go as planned. This story shows the power of perseverance and resilience. Another tale involves a player who became a leader by mentoring younger teammates. He shared his knowledge and experience, helping others succeed. His leadership and mentorship fostered an environment where everyone felt valued and supported.

These tales remind us of the importance of overcoming adversity and embracing change. Challenges are a part of life, but they don't have to hold us back. They can be stepping stones to success. Leadership and mentorship play crucial roles in fostering success, both on and off the field. By guiding others and sharing what we know, we can create a positive and supportive culture. This is true in football and in any area of life. The pioneers of the NFL showed us that with vision, dedication, and a willingness to innovate, we can achieve greatness.

As we look back on their contributions, we see how they have shaped the game we love today. Their legacy is a reminder that football is more than just a sport. It's a reflection of teamwork, perseverance, and a shared commitment to being the best. Their influence continues to inspire players, coaches, and fans around the world. As we move forward, we carry their lessons with us, ready to face new challenges and create the next chapter in football history.

CHAPTER 9
RISING STARS OF
THE GAME

9.1 TREVOR LAWRENCE: THE ROOKIE SENSATION

Trevor Lawrence is a quarterback who has quickly become a sensation in the world of football. His journey to the NFL began long before he wore the Jacksonville Jaguars' jersey. Trevor was a standout player even in high school. At Cartersville High

School in Georgia, he amazed everyone with his skills. He threw for over 13,000 yards and scored 161 touchdowns. These numbers made him one of the top recruits in the country. Colleges lined up to offer him a spot on their teams, but it was Clemson University where he chose to shine.

At Clemson, Trevor Lawrence showed just how talented he could be. He led the team to a National Championship as a freshman, a feat not many have achieved. His leadership and skill on the field were clear. He had a strong arm that could throw the ball far and with great accuracy. This made him a nightmare for opposing defenses. Lawrence could read defenses like a seasoned pro, making quick decisions on where to pass or when to run. His talent and hard work earned him the nickname "Sunshine," reflecting his bright future in football. With these skills, it was no surprise that he was a top pick in the NFL Draft.

When the Jacksonville Jaguars selected Trevor Lawrence with the number one overall pick in 2021, expectations were sky-high. Everyone hoped he would be the franchise quarterback who could turn the team's fortunes around. His first year in the NFL was filled with ups and downs. The transition from college to professional football is never easy. Lawrence faced challenges, including a tough schedule and a new level of competition. Still, he showed flashes of brilliance on the field. In some games, his passes were precise, and his leadership shone through. Fans saw moments of greatness that hinted at his potential to become one of the league's top quarterbacks.

Trevor Lawrence's potential for the future is something that excites both fans and experts alike. Many compare him to established quarterbacks who have made a significant impact in the NFL. His leadership qualities are evident, as he remains calm under pressure and inspires those around him. Lawrence has the potential to become the cornerstone of the Jacksonville Jaguars franchise. His ability to read defenses and make smart plays sets him apart from many other young quarterbacks. As he gains more experience, there is little doubt that he will continue to grow and improve. His journey in the NFL is just beginning, and the possibilities are endless.

Quick Quiz: Trevor's Talents

Think about Trevor Lawrence's journey to the NFL. What skills make him a standout quarterback? How did his college success prepare him for the challenges of professional football? Write down your thoughts and discuss them with a friend. Consider what qualities you admire most in Lawrence's story and how they can inspire you in your own pursuits.

9.2 CHASE YOUNG: A DEFENSIVE FORCE

Chase Young is so dominant that offenses fear him. His rise to NFL stardom started at Ohio State University, where he quickly became a standout. Young was a force on the field, making plays that left fans and coaches in awe. In 2019, he was a unanimous All-American, a rare honor that only the best college players earn. His talent and hard work also made him a finalist for the Heisman Trophy, a prestigious award usually reserved for offensive players. Young's college career was filled with moments that showcased his exceptional skills. He was known for his speed, power, and ability to disrupt opposing offenses. These qualities made him a top prospect for the NFL Draft.

Chase Young is a player who knows how to make an impact. On the field, he has an exceptional ability to rush the passer. This means he can quickly get past the offensive line and put pressure on the quarterback. His speed and strength make it hard for blockers to stop him. Young's presence alone can change how an offense plays. Teams have to plan around him, sometimes putting extra players to block his path. His tackles are powerful and precise. They often stop plays before they can develop. Young's sacks, where he tackles the quarterback behind the line of scrimmage, have influenced many games. Each time he takes down a quarterback, it shifts momentum in favor of his team.

Since entering the NFL, Young has collected several achievements and accolades. In his rookie season, he earned the NFL Defensive Rookie of the Year award. This honor shows how quickly he adapted to the professional level. It recognized his impact on the field and his ability to make big plays. He was also selected for the Pro Bowl as a young player, a nod to his talent and contributions to his team. These achievements highlight Young's dedication and skill as a defensive force. They also set the stage for what is sure to be a remarkable career. His ability to change the course of a game is something that fans and analysts admire.

Chase Young is not just a player but a leader. On the Washington Commanders, he has taken on a role that goes beyond just playing. He inspires his teammates with his work ethic and determination. Young's leadership is evident in how he carries himself on and off the field. He is someone that younger players look up to. They watch how he trains, plays, and interacts with others. His influence extends to defensive strategies as well. Coaches use his skills to develop plays that capitalize on his strengths. Young's presence on the team helps elevate everyone's performance. He is a player who can shape the future of defensive play in the NFL, making a lasting impact through both his actions and his leadership qualities.

9.3 JUSTIN JEFFERSON: THE NEW AGE RECEIVER

Catching a football in front of thousands of cheering fans, knowing history is being made, that's what Justin Jefferson experienced as he took the NFL by storm. His path to professional football began at Louisiana State University, where he quickly became a standout player. At LSU, Jefferson was part of a team that claimed a national title, thanks in part to his crucial performances. His ability to snag difficult catches and evade defenders made him a reliable target for his quarterback. Scouts noticed his talent, and it became clear that Jefferson was destined for the big leagues. When the Minnesota Vikings selected him in the NFL Draft, it was the beginning of an exciting new chapter in his life.

What makes Justin Jefferson a special receiver is his exceptional ability to run routes and catch the ball. Route-running might sound simple, but it's actually a skill that requires precision and timing. Jefferson moves with speed and agility, creating space between himself and the defenders. This separation is key. It gives him the chance to catch the ball without interference. His hands are steady and sure, allowing him to catch passes that seem impossible. Whether it's a short throw or a long bomb, Jefferson has a knack for being in the right place at the right time. This combination of skills sets him apart from many other receivers in the league.

In his early NFL seasons, Jefferson wasted no time making a name for himself. He broke records for rookie receiving yards, a testament to his talent and hard work. His performance caught the attention of fans and analysts alike. It wasn't long before he was selected for the Pro Bowl, an honor that highlights the best players each season. Jefferson's achievements didn't stop there. He also earned All-Pro honors, solidifying his status as one of the top receivers in the game. Each game, he continues to shine, showing the world what he's capable of. His early success is a sign of even greater things to come.

Jefferson's influence on the game goes beyond just his stats. Many compare him to legendary receivers from the past, those who have redefined what it means to be great. His style of play is changing how offenses approach the game. Coaches are using his skills to develop new strategies that maximize his impact. Jefferson's ability to stretch the field and create opportunities for his teammates is invaluable. As he continues to grow and develop, there's no telling what he'll achieve. With each game, he shows that the receiver position is evolving, and he's at the forefront of that change.

9.4 THE FUTURE IS BRIGHT: YOUNG STARS SHAPING THE NFL

Have you ever watched a player and thought they were going to change the game? That's exactly what many young players are doing in the NFL right now. Take Ja'Marr Chase, for example. He's a wide receiver for the Cincinnati Bengals, and people can't stop talking about him. He's fast, smart, and catches everything thrown his way. Then there's Micah Parsons, a linebacker for the Dallas Cowboys. He's known for his speed and ability to tackle anyone. Aidan Hutchinson, a defensive end for the Detroit Lions, is also making waves. He's strong and quick, making it hard for any offense to deal with him. And let's not forget Brock Purdy, George Kittle, and Justin Herbert. Each of these players brings something special to the field, and they're just getting started.

Young players like these are having a big impact on the NFL. They're bringing new energy and exciting play styles to the game. Their fresh approaches are changing how teams play. With their influence, games are going at a faster pace. There are more points being scored, and fans are loving it. These young stars are pushing the limits of what we think is possible in football. Their innovation is setting new trends, inspiring other players to try new things. This wave of youth is helping the NFL evolve into a more dynamic and thrilling sport to watch.

Mentorship plays a crucial role in the development of these young talents. Experienced players offer guidance and support, helping newcomers adjust to the professional league. Veterans like Tom Brady and Russell Wilson take time to mentor these rising stars, sharing their knowledge and experience. They teach them how to handle pressure and make smart decisions on the field. This support is invaluable, as it helps young players grow and improve. Within teams, you can find stories of mentorship and support. Older players take younger ones under their wing, helping them understand the game better. This creates a strong sense of camaraderie and teamwork, which is essential for success.

Looking ahead, these young players are poised to shape the future of the NFL in significant ways. They have the potential to create new rivalries, adding excitement to the league. As they continue to develop, we can expect record-breaking performances and unforgettable moments. The strategies teams use will also evolve. Coaches will adapt their plans to take advantage of the unique skills these players bring. Fans will engage more deeply with the sport, drawn in by the fast-paced action and innovative plays. The future of the NFL looks bright, with these young stars leading the way. As they continue to rise, they will inspire the next generation of players and fans alike, ensuring the game remains a beloved and thrilling part of our culture.

CHAPTER 10
NFL MATCHUPS AND RIVALRIES

10.1 RAIDERS VS STEELERS: A CLASH OF TITANS

Two great warriors prepare to clash on the battlefield. The air is thick with anticipation. This is what it feels like when the Raiders face off against the Steelers. Their rivalry is one of the fiercest in the NFL. It began on October 25, 1970, when the

Raiders beat the Steelers 31-14 at the Oakland-Alameda County Coliseum. But it wasn't until December 23, 1972, that this rivalry truly took off. This day is famous for a play called the "Immaculate Reception." During a playoff game, the Steelers were losing in the final seconds. Quarterback Terry Bradshaw threw a pass. It bounced off a defender and landed in the hands of Steelers' Franco Harris, who ran it for a touchdown. This miraculous play led the Steelers to a dramatic victory. It also sparked a fierce competitive streak between the two teams.

Throughout the 1970s, the Raiders and Steelers met in the playoffs for five straight seasons. This set an NFL record. These games were intense and hard-hitting. Both teams were among the best in the league. The 1976 AFC Championship Game stands out as one of the most memorable. The Steelers were missing some of their key players due to injuries. This gave the Raiders an advantage, and they won 24-7. Players like Terry Bradshaw and Ken Stabler delivered unforgettable performances during these clashes. Bradshaw, the Steelers' quarterback, was known for his powerful arm and quick thinking. On the Raiders' side, Stabler, nicknamed "The Snake," was cool under pressure and had a knack for making big plays. These players helped make the rivalry thrilling and unpredictable.

The rivalry between the Raiders and Steelers is more than just a series of games. It reflects broader cultural and regional differences. Pittsburgh is known for its blue-collar ethos. It is a city built on hard work and determination. The Steelers' playing style mirrors this, with a focus on tough defense and teamwork. On the other hand, the Raiders embodied the rebellious spirit of Oakland. They were known for their aggressive play and bold personalities. The team's image was one of defiance and grit. This contrast added an extra layer of excitement to every matchup. Fans from both sides took immense pride in their teams, creating a charged atmosphere at every game.

In recent years, the rivalry has evolved. Changes in team dynamics and player contributions have added new twists to the story. The Raiders, now based in Las Vegas, and the Steelers continue to deliver exciting games. In 2021, the Raiders won a thrilling match in Pittsburgh. Then, in 2023, the Steelers claimed victory in Las Vegas. These recent encounters show that the rivalry remains alive and well. Fans still look forward to these matchups, eager to see which team will come out on top. The rivalry's rich history and ongoing battles ensure its place as one of the NFL's most exciting.

Interactive Element: Rivalry Reflection

Think about what makes a rivalry special. Is it the history, the players, or the excitement of the games? Write down your thoughts or discuss with a friend. Imagine your favorite team in a rivalry game. How would you feel watching it? What moments would stand out to you? This exercise helps you appreciate the emotions and stories behind great football rivalries.

10.2 PACKERS VS. BEARS: THE CLASSIC SHOWDOWN

In 1921, when the Green Bay Packers and Chicago Bears first faced off, it marked the beginning of a rivalry that would become one of the NFL's most legendary matchups. Football during that time was a rough and rugged sport, and these two teams embodied that toughness. Over the decades, their games helped shape the NFL, highlighting fierce competition and a rich history. This rivalry has endured, growing in intensity and excitement with each season, becoming a cornerstone of the league.

Throughout the decades, memorable games have cemented the Packers-Bears rivalry as legendary. During the "Monsters of the Midway" era in the 1940s, the Bears' defense was so dominant that it struck fear in opposing teams. The Packers, however, often rose to the challenge, leading to intense battles on the field. Fast forward to the 1990s and early 2000s, where Brett Favre, the Packers' quarterback, delivered unforgettable performances against the Bears. Favre's ability to make big plays under pressure made him a thorn in the Bears' side. His rivalry with the Bears was marked by thrilling games and last-minute heroics, adding new chapters to this storied history.

For fans, the Packers vs. Bears rivalry is more than just a game; it's an experience. On game days, the excitement starts long before kickoff. At Lambeau Field in Green Bay, fans gather for tailgating, grilling burgers, and sharing stories of past games. Similarly, in Chicago, fans fill Soldier Field, creating a sea of navy blue and orange. The rivalry divides families and friends, each side passionately supporting their team. This rivalry has a profound impact on local communities, bringing people together in celebration or commiseration. It's a tradition that has been passed down through generations, strengthening bonds and community ties.

The Packers-Bears rivalry wouldn't be what it is without its legendary players and coaches. Vince Lombardi, the iconic Packers coach, brought a winning culture to Green Bay, leading the team to multiple championships. His rival, George Halas, was the founder and longtime coach of the Bears. Halas was known for his fierce competitiveness and innovative strategies. Their battles on the sidelines added another layer of drama to the rivalry. Players like Walter Payton, the legendary Bears running back, dazzled with his incredible skills and sportsmanship. Meanwhile, Bart Starr, the Packers' star quarterback, led his team with grace and precision. These figures have left lasting legacies, inspiring new generations of players and fans alike.

The stories from this rivalry are endless, and they continue to grow with each game. The Packers and Bears have faced each other over 200 times, making it the most-played rivalry in NFL history. Each matchup adds new tales of triumph and heartbreak, with both teams striving to add another win to their storied records. The rivalry's longevity is a testament to its special place in football history. As fans eagerly anticipate each encounter, they know they're witnessing a part of NFL tradition. The Packers vs. Bears rivalry is more than a game; it's a celebration of football's rich history and the passion it inspires.

10.3 COWBOYS VS. 49ERS: BATTLES FOR THE AGES

Two teams with deep-rooted histories and a fierce desire to win come together: the Cowboys versus the 49ers. Their rivalry gained intensity in the 1980s and 1990s when both teams were at their peak. Frequent playoff clashes put everything on the line, with the Cowboys led by legendary coach Tom Landry, known for his strategic precision, and the 49ers under Bill Walsh, whose innovative West Coast offense revolutionized the game. These matchups created some of the most memorable moments in NFL history, establishing one of the league's greatest rivalries.

One game that stands out in this rivalry is the 1982 NFC Championship. It featured a moment known as "The Catch." The 49ers were trailing with little time left. Joe Montana, their quarterback, threw a high pass. Dwight Clark leaped into the air and caught it, scoring a touchdown. This play led the 49ers to victory and marked the changing of the guard in the NFC. Another key moment came in the 1994 NFC Championship. This time, Steve Young, a 49ers quarterback, faced Troy Aikman of the Cowboys.

Young led the 49ers to a win, cementing his place as one of the best. These games were more than just wins and losses. They were turning points that defined the rivalry and the teams' legacies.

The Cowboys and 49ers rivalry is not just about football. It reflects broader cultural themes and regional pride. The Cowboys are often called "America's Team." Their fans are everywhere, and they have a rich tradition of winning. The 49ers, based on the West Coast, are known for their dominance during the 1980s. They brought a new style of play with their West Coast offense, focusing on short passes and precision. This clash of styles and identities adds depth to their matchups. Every game feels like a battle for more than just points. It is about pride, tradition, and who will come out on top in the end.

As we look back at this rivalry, we see how it has influenced NFL history. The legendary matchups between these two teams have shaped the league's narrative. They pushed each other to be better, raising the level of competition. The intense games and unforgettable moments have inspired new generations of players and fans. They have also influenced modern rivalries. Teams today still look to the Cowboys and 49ers as examples of excellence and determination. This rivalry has shown that great teams and great games are built on passion, strategy, and a desire to be the best.

10.4 RIVALRY WEEK: THE STORIES BEHIND THE GAMES

Every season, NFL fans look forward to something special— Rivalry Week. This isn't just any week. It's a time when some of the fiercest NFL matchups take center stage. Teams with long-standing rivalries face off, bringing an extra layer of excitement to the games. These rivalries capture the imagination of fans, driving them to stadiums in droves. They cheer for their favorite teams with unmatched enthusiasm. The energy is electric. Rivalry Week is a big deal because it highlights the passion and history between teams. Fans show up in huge numbers, making the games even more thrilling. This extra excitement helps boost attendance and creates an atmosphere that players thrive in. The whole experience is unforgettable.

What makes rivalry games stand out? It's the intensity. There's a competitive spirit that isn't always present in regular games. Players give their all, knowing how much these wins mean to their fans. Every yard gained, every tackle made, feels more important. The stakes are higher, and the pressure is on. Teams want to prove they are the best. The atmosphere is charged, and the action on the field reflects that. Players often find an extra gear, pushing themselves to perform at their best. Rivalry games are about pride and proving who comes out on top. It's a battle where every play matters, and the tension keeps everyone on the edge of their seats.

Among these intense battles, stories of unlikely heroes often emerge. Sometimes, it's a player who hasn't seen much action all season. They suddenly step up and make a game-changing play. These underdog victories are memorable. They remind us that anyone can rise to the occasion when it matters most. Take, for instance, a backup quarterback who throws a last-minute touchdown. Or a rookie kicker who nails a winning field goal. Their performances become legendary. Fans talk about these moments for years to come. These stories show that in rivalry games, anything can happen. They inspire young fans to believe in themselves and their abilities. They remind us all that in football, every player has the potential to be a hero.

Media and fan culture play a huge role in building the hype around rivalries. Social media platforms buzz with predictions and discussions. Fans share their thoughts on who will win and why. They post photos and videos, adding to the excitement. Fan forums light up with debates and friendly banter. This online chatter helps set the stage for the games, fueling anticipation. Team traditions and rituals also add to the buildup. Think of the chants, the songs, and the colorful banners. These rituals are passed down from one generation of fans to the next. They create a sense of belonging and community. The media picks up on these stories, broadcasting them to a wider audience. They highlight the passion of the fans, making the games feel even more special.

As Rivalry Week unfolds, fans are treated to a spectacle unlike any other. The stories behind the games add depth and meaning to each matchup. With the final whistle, a new chapter is added to the rich history of these rivalries. The games may end, but the memories last a lifetime. Fans continue to share stories of their favorite moments, keeping the spirit alive. They look forward to the next time their teams will meet, ready to cheer them on once again. The excitement of Rivalry Week reminds us why we love football. It connects us, fuels our passion, and leaves us eager for more. As we turn our attention to the next chapter, we'll explore the teams and players who have made history with unforgettable moments and legendary plays.

CHAPTER 11
GREAT MOMENTS IN FOOTBALL

11.1 THE IMMACULATE RECEPTION: A PLAY FOR THE AGES

The game has only seconds left on the clock. The crowd is on the edge of their seats. The team with the ball needs a miracle to win. Suddenly, a play unfolds that will be talked about for decades. This is exactly what happened during the Immaculate Reception in 1972. The game was an AFC Divisional Playoff between the Pittsburgh Steelers and the Oakland Raiders. It was a cold day in Pittsburgh, and the stakes were high. Both teams fought hard, and the score was low. The Raiders led 7-6 with just 22 seconds remaining. The Steelers faced a crucial fourth-and-10 situation from their own 40-yard line. They needed a big play to keep their playoff hopes alive.

Terry Bradshaw, the Steelers' quarterback, took the snap. The Raiders' defense came rushing at him. He dodged and weaved, trying to find an open receiver. With defenders closing in, Bradshaw launched the football downfield. The pass was intended for John "Frenchy" Fuqua, but it never reached him. The ball collided with the helmet of Raiders defender Jack Tatum, or perhaps Fuqua's shoulder pads. It flew into the air, seemingly out of reach for any player. But then, as if guided by fate, Franco Harris appeared. He scooped the ball just inches above the turf. Harris sprinted down the sideline, dodging tackles, and scored a touchdown. The crowd erupted in cheers. The Steelers had won with a final score of 13-7. It was a moment no one would soon forget.

The play was incredible, but it also sparked controversy. Some people questioned whether the ball had hit the ground before Harris caught it. Others debated if it had touched Fuqua or Tatum first. At that time, NFL rules stated that a pass could only be legally caught if it touched an offensive player first, then a defensive player. The officials on the field conferred and decided the play was legal. The Immaculate Reception stood, and the Steelers celebrated their victory. But the debates continued in the days and years that followed. Fans and analysts argued over replays, trying to determine the truth. Despite the controversy, the play remains one of the most famous in NFL history.

The Immaculate Reception had a huge impact on the Steelers. It was the beginning of their rise as a dominant team in the 1970s. Before this game, the Steelers had never won a playoff game. This victory gave them the confidence and momentum they needed. They went on to win four Super Bowl titles in the coming decade. The play changed how people viewed the Steelers. They were no longer underdogs. They became a powerhouse team with a reputation for making big plays when it mattered most.

This moment is a symbol of hope and determination. It shows that anything is possible, even when the odds seem stacked against you. The Immaculate Reception is replayed on highlight reels every year. It serves as a reminder of the magic that can happen in football. Fans still talk about it, and young players dream of making their own incredible plays. The legacy of the Immaculate Reception lives on, inspiring future generations to strive for greatness on the field. The story of this play is a testament to the excitement and unpredictability of the NFL, where heroes emerge and legends are born in the blink of an eye.

Reflection: What Would You Do?

Think about yourself in Franco Harris's shoes. The ball is flying through the air. Your team needs you to catch it. How would you feel in that moment? Write down your thoughts or share them with a friend. Consider the bravery and quick thinking needed to make such a play. Would you have the courage to go for it? Reflect on what it takes to stay calm and focused in high-pressure situations.

11.2 THE MUSIC CITY MIRACLE: UNBELIEVABLE COMEBACKS

It's a crisp January day in Nashville, Tennessee. The year is 2000, and the Tennessee Titans are about to face the Buffalo Bills in the AFC Wild Card playoff game. The stakes are sky-high, with both teams eyeing a spot in the divisional round. It was a closely fought battle, as both sides had played their hearts out, with neither willing to give an inch. The game had been tense from the start, with each team showcasing their strengths. The Titans, known for their powerful running game, went head-to-head against the Bills, who countered with a strong defense. As the clock ticked down, the Bills took a late lead with a field goal, making the score 16-15 in their favor. The Titans had only seconds left to change their fate.

With the game on the line, the Titans lined up for the kickoff. The pressure was immense. Fans held their breath, hoping for a miracle. What followed would become one of the most talked-about plays in NFL history. Lorenzo Neal, a fullback for the Titans, caught the kickoff and immediately handed the ball to Frank Wycheck. Wycheck, a tight end known for his smart play, quickly looked for an opportunity. He saw Kevin Dyson, a wide receiver, on the opposite side of the field. In one swift motion, Wycheck threw the ball across the field to Dyson. This lateral pass was risky, but it was their only chance. Dyson caught the ball and sprinted down the sideline. Titans players and fans erupted as he raced 75 yards into the end zone. The crowd went wild. It was a touchdown, and the Titans had pulled off an amazing win, with a final score of 22-16.

The aftermath of the Music City Miracle was just as dramatic as the play itself. Titans fans were ecstatic, celebrating the unexpected victory. They cheered, hugged, and reveled in the moment. It was a feeling of pure joy. On the other hand, Bills supporters were left in disbelief. They couldn't believe what had just happened. Many were stunned, struggling to understand how their team had lost in such a surprising way. The play quickly became a hot topic of discussion. People questioned whether Wycheck's lateral pass had been legal. Some argued that it was a forward pass, which would have made it illegal. The referees reviewed the play. They watched it from every angle and concluded that the pass had been a legal lateral. The ruling stood, but debates about the play continued to spark conversations among fans and analysts alike.

The Music City Miracle had a lasting impact on the Titans' season and NFL history. The thrilling win gave the Titans a huge momentum boost. It energized the team and their fans, propelling them through the playoffs. With newfound confidence, the Titans went on to defeat the Indianapolis Colts and the Jacksonville Jaguars in subsequent playoff games. They reached Super Bowl XXXIV, where they faced the St. Louis Rams. Although the Titans fell short in the final seconds of the Super Bowl, their journey to the championship game was unforgettable. The Music City Miracle became a defining moment in the Titans' franchise history, symbolizing hope, determination, and the magic of football. It showed that no game is over until the final whistle blows, and that miracles can happen when you least expect them. The story of this play continues to inspire players and fans, reminding them of the thrill and unpredictability of the sport.

11.3 THE CATCH: A MOMENT OF MAGIC

A football game that could determine a trip to the Super Bowl creates a tense atmosphere, with fans filled with excitement. This was the scene during the 1981 NFC Championship Game between the San Francisco 49ers and the Dallas Cowboys. At the time, the

Cowboys were known for their dominance and strong performances, while the 49ers were building a promising future. With a Super Bowl berth on the line, the stakes were high for both teams. The fierce rivalry between these squads only heightened the drama, as neither was willing to back down after fighting hard to reach this moment.

As the clock ticked down in the final minutes, the tension grew even more. The 49ers trailed by six points. They needed a touchdown to take the lead and secure their spot in the Super Bowl. The ball was in the hands of their quarterback, Joe Montana. Known for his calm under pressure, he had one last chance to win the game. Montana took the snap and quickly found himself in trouble. The Cowboys' defense was closing in fast. He scrambled to his right, looking for an open receiver. As he neared the sideline, Montana spotted Dwight Clark in the back of the end zone. With defenders all around, Montana threw the ball high, hoping for a miracle. Clark leaped into the air, extending his arms as far as they could go. He snatched the ball out of the sky with his fingertips, landing gracefully in the end zone. The stadium erupted. The 49ers had scored a touchdown. They took the lead and eventually won the game 28-27.

This play, known as "The Catch," became a turning point for the 49ers. It marked the beginning of a new era for the team. Before this moment, the 49ers had struggled to find success. They had never won a Super Bowl. But "The Catch" changed everything. It gave them the confidence they needed. The play showed they could compete with the best and come out on top. This victory launched the 49ers into a dynasty. They went on to win four Super Bowls in the 1980s. Joe Montana and their coach, Bill Walsh, became legends. People began to see them as two of the greatest minds in football. "The Catch" was the moment that put them on the map.

In the years that followed, "The Catch" remained a symbol of greatness. It showed what was possible when players stayed cool under pressure. Montana's calm decision-making and Clark's incredible focus were the keys to this success. The play is often mentioned in discussions about the best moments in NFL history. It reminds fans and players alike that anything can happen. Even when the odds seem against you, there's always a chance for victory. "The Catch" is a shining example of this belief. It's a testament to the power of teamwork, trust, and determination.

The legacy of "The Catch" goes beyond just one game or one season. It inspired a generation of fans and players. Many young athletes grew up dreaming of making their own game-winning plays. Coaches studied the 49ers' strategies, hoping to replicate their success. The play is replayed every year, reminding new fans of its magic. "The Catch" taught us that football is not just about physical skill. It's also about heart, courage, and the ability to rise above challenges. This moment will forever hold a special place in the hearts of football lovers, symbolizing the thrill and wonder of the game.

As we reach the end of this chapter, think about how these great NFL moments have shaped the league. They've given us unforgettable memories and taught us valuable lessons. From amazing catches to last-second victories, these plays remind us why we love football. They show us that with hard work and belief, anything is possible. Next, we'll explore more incredible stories that continue to inspire and captivate fans everywhere.

CHAPTER 12
INSPIRATIONAL FOOTBALL TALES

12.1 KURT WARNER: FROM GROCERY STORE TO SUPER BOWL MVP

K urt Warner went from stocking shelves in a grocery store to shining under the bright lights of a Super Bowl. This might sound like a fairy tale, but it is a real-life story. Before he became a famous quarterback, Warner faced many challenges. He worked at a Hy-Vee supermarket, stacking cans and helping customers. It was a tough job, and he often wondered if his dream of playing football at the highest level would ever come true. But Warner didn't give up. He kept practicing, believing that his chance would come.

Warner's journey took a turn when he joined the Arena Football League. This league is different from the NFL. It has a smaller field and faster games. Warner played for the Iowa Barnstormers, and his talent began to shine. People started to notice his quick passes and sharp decisions. Playing in the Arena League helped Warner improve his skills. It taught him how to handle pressure and lead a team. These experiences became stepping stones on his path to the NFL. His time in the arena gave him the confidence to keep pushing forward.

In 1998, Warner signed with the St. Louis Rams. At first, he was not the starting quarterback. He watched and learned from the sidelines, waiting for his moment. That moment came in 1999 when the Rams' starting quarterback, Trent Green, got injured. Warner stepped up to fill the gap. Many doubted if he could handle the pressure, but Warner was ready. He took charge and led the Rams with determination. Under his leadership, the team became known as the "Greatest Show on Turf." Their offense dazzled fans with fast-paced plays and high scores.

Warner's performance was nothing short of spectacular. He led the Rams to victory in Super Bowl XXXIV, earning the title of Super Bowl MVP. His story captivated the world. Warner became a symbol of perseverance and triumph. He didn't just stop there. He also won the NFL MVP award twice. His achievements showed that hard work and belief in yourself can lead to incredible success. Warner set records for passing touchdowns and yards, proving that he was one of the best in the game.

Warner's legacy extends beyond his stats and awards. He has inspired countless players who were once overlooked or undrafted. These players see his journey and believe that they, too, can make it big. Warner became a mentor to young quarterbacks, sharing his insights and experiences. After retiring, he continued to influence the game as an analyst. He helps fans understand the strategies and skills involved in football. Warner's story reminds us that no dream is too big. With dedication and a little help, anything is possible.

Reflection: Your Own Path

Think about a time when you faced a challenge. How did you overcome it? Write down your thoughts or share them with a friend. Consider how Warner's story of perseverance might inspire you in your own life. Reflect on the qualities that helped him succeed and how you can apply them to pursue your dreams.

12.2 DOUG FLUTIE: PROVING THE DOUBTERS WRONG

Doug Flutie faced skepticism from the start. Critics doubted his abilities due to his height. Standing at just 5 feet 10 inches, he was shorter than most quarterbacks. Many thought he wouldn't succeed in professional football. They believed he was too small to see over the offensive line and deliver accurate throws. Despite these doubts, Flutie remained determined. He trusted in his skills and refused to let others define him. His playing style was also different. He relied on quick thinking and mobility to outmaneuver defenders. Some saw this as unconventional, but for Flutie, it was simply how he played best.

Flutie's college years were a different story. He attended Boston College, where he quickly made a name for himself. His college career reached a peak during a game against the Miami Hurricanes. With seconds left, Boston College was trailing. Flutie took the snap and scrambled out of the pocket. He launched the ball 63 yards into the end zone. It was a risky pass, known as a "Hail Mary." Everyone held their breath. Gerard Phelan, his receiver, caught the ball, securing an unexpected victory. This play, known as the "Hail Flutie," became legendary. It showed Flutie's ability to perform under pressure and his knack for making big plays.

Despite this success, NFL teams overlooked Flutie in the draft. He faced an uphill battle to prove himself. Instead of giving up, he took his talents to the Canadian Football League (CFL). There, he thrived. He played with the BC Lions, Calgary Stampeders, and Toronto Argonauts. Flutie led his teams to multiple championships, becoming a star in the league. His success in Canada showed the world he was more than capable of leading a team. It also helped him develop his skills further, preparing him for another shot at the NFL.

Flutie's chance to return to the NFL came with the Buffalo Bills. He joined the team and quickly proved he still had what it took. His time in the CFL had honed his skills, making him a more mature and confident player. Flutie's mobility and improvisation on the field were key factors in his success. He could escape pressure and make plays that seemed impossible. This made him a fan favorite and a nightmare for defenses. After the Bills, he continued his career with the New England Patriots, further cementing his place in the NFL.

Flutie's legacy goes beyond his statistics. He changed how people viewed quarterbacks. Before him, many believed only tall quarterbacks could succeed. Flutie showed that talent and heart mattered more than size. His style of play paved the way for smaller quarterbacks. They saw his success and knew they could follow in his footsteps. Flutie became a symbol of perseverance and innovation. He inspired a generation of players who use mobility and quick thinking to excel. His impact on the game is still felt today, as more teams embrace versatile and agile quarterbacks.

Flutie's story teaches an important lesson. It shows that with determination and hard work, you can overcome any obstacle. He faced doubts and criticism but never let them stop him. Instead, he used them as motivation to become better. His career is a testament to the power of belief in oneself. Flutie proved that no matter what others say, you can achieve great things if you stay true to yourself. His journey is a reminder that sometimes, the most unconventional paths lead to the greatest successes.

12.3 MICHAEL OHER: THE BLIND SIDE STORY

Michael Oher's life began with challenges that seemed insurmountable. Growing up in poverty, he faced many hurdles that could have stopped him from succeeding. His family situation was unstable. His mother struggled with addiction, and his father was not around. This left Michael without the support most kids rely on. He often found himself without a consistent place to call home. Homelessness was a constant threat. Moving from one place to another, he lacked the stability needed for growth and development. Education was another challenge. Constant moving meant he attended several schools, each with different expectations and environments. This made it hard for him to keep up with his studies. Despite these obstacles, Michael held onto a hope that his life could be different.

The turning point in Michael's life came when he met the Tuohy family. They saw potential in him that others had overlooked. The Tuohys provided Michael with a stable home and the support he desperately needed. They encouraged him to focus on his education and his love for football. With their help, Michael began to thrive. At Briarcrest Christian School, he developed into a standout offensive lineman. His natural talent, combined with hard work, caught the attention of college scouts. The Tuohys' belief in him was a catalyst for change. They showed him that he was capable of achieving great things. This support opened doors that once seemed closed.

Michael's talents on the field led him to the University of Mississippi, where he continued to excel. He became one of the top offensive linemen in college football. His strength and skill made him a key player for his team. His hard work paid off when he was selected in the first round of the NFL Draft by the Baltimore Ravens. This was a dream come true for Michael. He achieved something remarkable, considering where he started. His success continued in the NFL, where he helped the Ravens win a Super Bowl. His journey from hardship to triumph is a testament to his resilience and determination.

Michael's story has had a broader impact beyond the football field. It inspired the book and film "The Blind Side," which brought his life story to a global audience. The film highlighted the relationship between Michael and the Tuohy family. It showed how love and support could change a life. This story resonated with many people, shedding light on the importance of family and community. Michael's journey has also sparked conversations about adoption and mentorship. He has become an advocate for these causes, using his platform to encourage others to give back and support those in need. His story reminds us that everyone has the potential to succeed, given the right opportunities and support.

12.4 UNYIELDING SPIRIT: TALES OF TRIUMPH OVER ADVERSITY

In the world of football, the field isn't just a place where games are played. It's also where some of the most inspiring stories unfold. These stories often begin with setbacks. Many stars have faced serious injuries that could have ended their careers. Yet, they chose to fight back, showing incredible strength and determination. Take Adrian Peterson, for example. He tore his ACL, a major ligament in the knee, during a game. Such an injury is often career-threatening for athletes. But Peterson's story is one of resilience. He worked tirelessly through physical therapy and training. His hard work paid off. He returned to the field stronger than ever, achieving an MVP season shortly after his recovery. His tale shows what can be achieved when you refuse to give up.

Injuries aren't the only challenges players face. Many deal with personal struggles off the field. Brandon Marshall is one player who has openly shared his battles with mental health. Early in his career, Marshall faced personal challenges that affected his performance and life. Instead of hiding, he sought help and began advocating for mental health awareness. His courage to speak out helped reduce stigma around mental health issues in the sports world. Marshall's journey highlights the power of perseverance and redemption. It shows that facing your struggles head-on can lead to personal growth and positive change. His advocacy has inspired many, proving that even in tough times, there is always hope for a better future.

Team support and mentorship play crucial roles in a player's success. Behind every great player is often a group of teammates and coaches offering guidance and encouragement. These mentors help young players navigate the challenges of professional sports. They provide wisdom and support, teaching valuable skills both on and off the field. Veterans often take rookies under their wing, sharing experiences and advice. This bond creates a strong team dynamic, where everyone works together towards a common goal. The encouragement from teammates can boost confidence and help players overcome obstacles. Mentorship fosters a sense of belonging, showing young athletes that they are never alone in their journey.

These stories teach us important lessons about resilience. They show that success doesn't come easy. It requires hard work, determination, and the courage to keep pushing forward, no matter the odds. Whether it's recovering from an injury, overcoming personal challenges, or relying on team support, these tales remind us of the power of persistence. They inspire us to pursue our dreams, even when faced with difficulties. The path may be tough, but with resilience, anything is possible. These lessons extend beyond sports. They encourage you to apply the same determination in your own life. No obstacle is too big if you believe in yourself and keep moving forward.

As we reflect on these powerful stories, we see the bigger picture of what it means to be a part of this great game. It's more than just winning games or setting records. It's about the journey and the growth that comes with it. It's about the friendships and bonds formed along the way. These tales of triumph over adversity connect us all, inspiring us to be the best versions of ourselves. They remind us that with heart and determination, we can overcome any challenge.

LOVE THE BOOK?
HERE'S HOW YOU CAN HELP!

If you or your child enjoy *A Kid's Guide to Football Legends*, we'd love to hear your thoughts! Leaving a review on Amazon is a great way to support me and share your feedback with others. By leaving a review, you're helping other young readers discover this fantastic book.

How to Leave a ★★★★★ Review on Amazon

1. **Go to the Amazon page** for *A Kid's Guide to Football Legends*.
2. Scroll down to the "Customer Reviews" section.
3. Click on the "Write a Customer Review" button.
4. Share what you loved about the book – Was it the inspiring stories? The legendary players?
5. Hit "Submit" – And that's it!

Don't Wait – Share Your Thoughts Today!

CONCLUSION

You've taken a journey through the exciting world of football. Along the way, you discovered how the sport came to be, learned about legendary players, and relived unforgettable moments. This book has shown you the power of dreams, hard work, and the spirit of the game. Each chapter offered a glimpse into what makes football so special. From the birth of the league to the inspiring stories of its players, you explored a rich history filled with triumphs and challenges.

The stories of Tom Brady, Walter Payton, and so many others teach us important lessons. They remind us of the value of perseverance and teamwork. They show how the right mindset can overcome any obstacle. You learned about the importance of sportsmanship and how players have used their fame to give back to their communities. These lessons are not just for football. You can apply them to any part of your life. They encourage you to chase your dreams and work hard for what you believe in.

Football is more than just a game. It brings people together. It creates moments of joy and excitement. Families gather to watch games, friends cheer on their favorite teams, and communities unite in support of their local heroes. Football teaches us about dedication, effort, and the thrill of competition. It inspires people of all ages to push their limits and strive for greatness. Whether you're on the field or cheering from the stands, the game has a place for everyone.

As you close this book, think about how you can bring these lessons into your life. Maybe you want to play football, join a local team, or just learn more about the game. Whatever your path, remember that the qualities you admired in the players can guide you too. Be determined, work well with others, and never give up on your goals. Support your friends and community, just like your favorite players do on and off the field.

Thank you for joining me on this journey. Your curiosity and enthusiasm make the world of Football even more exciting. I hope this book has sparked your interest and inspired you to keep exploring. The world of football is vast, with so much more to learn and discover.

Stay connected with the game by watching current matches, learning about new players, and maybe even playing yourself. Read more about the history and stories of football. Join local leagues or teams if you can. These activities will deepen your understanding and love for the sport.

Remember, the lessons from this book are not just about football. They are about life. Keep dreaming big and working hard. Believe in yourself and your abilities. You can achieve anything you set your mind to. Just like the players you've read about, you have the power to inspire others and make a difference.

Continue to explore, learn, and grow. The world is full of opportunities, and your journey is just beginning. Keep striving for excellence, both on and off the field. Your passion and dedication will lead you to great things.

REFERENCES

History of American football. (n.d.). *Wikipedia.* https://en.wikipedia.org/wiki/History_of_American_football

Walter Camp Football Foundation. (n.d.). *Walter Camp Football Foundation.* https://waltercamp.org/pages/about/walter-camp/

Pro Football Hall of Fame. (2005, January). Sept. 17, 1920 -- The founding of the NFL. *Pro Football Hall of Fame.* https://www.profootballhof.com/news/2005/01/news-sept-17-1920-the-founding-of-the-nfl/

NFL Explained: Innovation in player health and safety. (n.d.). *NFL.* https://www.nfl.com/playerhealthandsafety/equipment-and-innovation/aws-partnership/nflexplainedinnovation

Youth and high school tackle football glossary. (n.d.). *NFL.* https://playfootball.nfl.com/resources/youth-and-high-school-tackle-football-glossary/

The history of football uniforms. (2019, December 12). *NPP.* https://mynpp.com/blog/2019/12/12/the-history-of-football-uniforms/

American football positions facts for kids. (n.d.). *Kiddle.* https://kids.kiddle.co/American_football_positions

Formations 101. (n.d.). *NFL Operations.* https://operations.nfl.com/learn-the-game/nfl-basics/formations-101/

Horowitz, D. (2021, February 8). How Tom Brady overcame adversity to be a 7x Super Bowl champion. *Medium.* https://medium.com/@david.horowitz/how-tom-brady-overcame-adversity-to-be-a-7x-super-bowl-champion-3ed98acfea67

The official site of Jerry Rice. (n.d.). *Jerry Rice Football.* https://www.jerryricefootball.com/about

OzzyCollectibleHub. (2020, December 2). Walter Payton: The legend of Sweetness. *Medium.* https://medium.com/@ozzycollectiblehub/walter-payton-the-legend-of-sweetness-d8f7ad635855

Legendary NFL players and their impact on the game. (n.d.). *XFL News Hub.* https://xflnewshub.com/extra/legendary-nfl-players-and-their-impact-on-the-game/

Patrick Mahomes. (n.d.). *Wikipedia.* https://en.wikipedia.org/wiki/Patrick_Mahomes

Aaron Donald's workout: The all-star defensive tackle's routine. (n.d.). *SET FOR*

SET. https://www.setforset.com/blogs/news/aaron-donald-workout?srsltid= AfmBOoqk2uiFb9AfnKuedhBMMYvg3YPqpnPiLLS-bskPI3Sy7aQYzyYQ

Why Not You Foundation. (n.d.). *Why Not You Foundation.* https://whynotyoufd n.org/

Inspire change | NFL social justice initiative. (n.d.). *NFL.* https://www.nfl.com/ causes/inspire-change/

William Perry (American football). (n.d.). *Wikipedia.* https://en.wikipedia.org/wiki/ William_Perry_(American_football)

Rob Gronkowski bio & career accomplishments. (n.d.). *Fox Sports.* https://www. foxsports.com/personalities/rob-gronkowski/bio

Bowen, M. (2013, June 17). Breaking down Vince Wilfork's impact on the New England Patriots' defense. *Bleacher Report.* https://bleacherreport.com/articles/ 1673985-breaking-down-vince-wilforks-impact-on-the-new-england-patriots-defense

Physiological demands of American football. (n.d.). *Gatorade Sports Science Institute.* http://www.gssiweb.org/sports-science-exchange/article/sse-143-physiologi cal-demands-of-american-football

Steel Curtain. (n.d.). *Wikipedia.* https://en.wikipedia.org/wiki/Steel_Curtain#:~

Ray Lewis. (n.d.). *Pro Football Hall of Fame.* https://www.profootballhof.com/play ers/ray-lewis/

Deion Sanders. (n.d.). *Wikipedia.* https://en.wikipedia.org/wiki/Deion_Sanders

10 greatest defenses in NFL history. (n.d.). *Athlon Sports.* https://athlonsports.com/ nfl/10-greatest-defenses-nfl-history

Peyton Manning. (n.d.). *Wikipedia.* https://en.wikipedia.org/wiki/Peyton_Man ning#:~:text=Manning%20holds%20many%20N-FL%20records,yards%20and%20career%20passing%20touchdowns.

Pro Football Hall of Fame. (2024, March 4). Gold Jacket Spotlight: Barry Sanders played with style of his own. *Pro Football Hall of Fame.* https://www.profootball hof.com/news/2024/03/gold-jacket-spotlight-barry-sanders-played-with-style-of-his-own/#:~

Randy Moss. (n.d.). *Pro Football Hall of Fame.* https://www.profootballhof.com/play ers/randy-moss/#:~

CyberGhost VPN. (2023, February 2). The greatest NFL plays of all time from all 32 teams. *CyberGhost Privacy Hub.* https://www.cyberghostvpn.com/privacy hub/best-nfl-plays-in-history/

Vince Lombardi | Official website | Football coaching. (n.d.). *Vince Lombardi.* https://vincelombardi.com/

Paul Brown. (n.d.). *Wikipedia.* https://en.wikipedia.org/wiki/Paul_Brown#:~

West Coast offense. (n.d.). *Wikipedia.* https://en.wikipedia.org/wiki/West_Coast_of fense#:~:

Archer, T. (2024, February 10). The NFL's African-American pioneers produced many milestones, fewer memories. *Dallas Morning News*. https://www.dallas news.com/sports/cowboys/2024/02/10/the-nfls-african-american-pioneers-produced-many-milestones-fewer-memories/

Johnson, L. (2022, June 20). Watch: Best highlights from Trevor Lawrence's rookie season. *USA Today: Draft Wire*. https://draftwire.usatoday.com/2022/06/20/nfl-trevor-lawrence-highlights-jacksonville-jaguars-2021/

Chase Young - 2019-20 football roster. (n.d.). *Ohio State Athletics*. https://ohiostate buckeyes.com/sports/football/roster/chase-young/456

Vikings WR Justin Jefferson sets rookie record for most receiving yards. (n.d.). *NFL*. https://www.nfl.com/news/vikings-wr-justin-jefferson-sets-rookie-record-for-most-receiving-yards

2023 Rising Stars List. (n.d.). *NFLPA*. https://nflpa.com/partners/posts/2023-rising-stars-list

Raiders–Steelers rivalry. (n.d.). *American Football Wiki*. https://americanfootball.fandom.com/wiki/Raiders%E2%80%93Steelers_rivalry

Demovsky, R. (2019, December 4). 10 of the most memorable games in the Packers-Bears rivalry. *Packers News*. https://www.packersnews.com/story/sports/nfl/packers/2019/12/04/packers-bears-rivalry-ten-memorable-games/2095498001/

USA Today Sports. (2023, January 20). Cowboys vs. 49ers: Greatest all-time NFL playoff games. *USA Today*. https://www.usatoday.com/story/sports/nfl/2023/01/20/cowboys-niners-rivalry-nfl-playoffs-greatest-games/11070811002/#:~:text=1981%20NFC%20champi-onship%20game%20(',start%20of%20the%2049ers'%20dynasty.

The impact of the phenomenon of sport rivalry on fans. (n.d.). *Journal of Transformative Works and Cultures*. https://journal.transformativeworks.org/index.php/twc/article/view/1607/1963

Pro Football Hall of Fame. (n.d.). The Immaculate Reception: Catch of a lifetime. *Pro Football Hall of Fame*. https://www.profootballhof.com/football-history/the-immaculate-reception-catch-of-a-lifetime/

Sporting News. (2022, January 8). Music City Miracle, revisited: The story of Frank Wycheck's lateral pass controversy. *Sporting News*. https://www.sportingnews.com/us/nfl/news/music-city-miracle-frank-wycheck-titans-bills-lateral-pass-controversy/3bb45f715a7e9c474b1efacf

The Catch (American football). (n.d.). *Wikipedia*. https://en.wikipedia.org/wiki/The_Catch_(American_football)

Private Internet Access. (n.d.). 10 most iconic moments in NFL history. *Private Internet Access*. https://www.privateinternetaccess.com/blog/greatest-nfl-moments/

Pro Football Hall of Fame. (n.d.). Kurt Warner. *Pro Football Hall of Fame*. https://www.profootballhof.com/players/kurt-warner/

Hail Flutie. (n.d.). *Wikipedia*. https://en.wikipedia.org/wiki/Hail_Flutie

Biography.com Editors. (n.d.). The true story of Michael Oher and 'The Blind Side'. *Biography.com*. https://www.biography.com/movies-tv/the-blind-side-true-story-michael-oher

Yardbarker Staff. (2020, August 14). NFL players who returned from devastating injuries. *Yardbarker*. https://www.yardbarker.com/nfl/articles/nfl_players_who_returned_from_devastating_injuries/s1__33229937

AUTHOR BIO

Kent Jameson grew up in a quaint farm town in Iowa, where he developed a deep appreciation for the simplicity of rural life. In 1994, he earned a Bachelor of Science degree in Family and Consumer Sciences Journalism from Iowa State University.

When he's not writing, Kent enjoys spending time with his two sons, often cheering them on from the sidelines as they play basketball. Currently residing in Phoenix, Arizona, he continues to live by the small-town values that have guided him throughout his life and career.

www.ingramcontent.com/pod-product-compliance
Lightning Source LLC
LaVergne TN
LVHW051418080426
835508LV00022B/3144